69-12651 (12-9-69)

# Three-Fifths of a Man

# THREE-FIFTHS
# OF A MAN

FLOYD McKISSICK

*The Macmillan Company*

*Collier-Macmillan Ltd., London*

The Macmillan Company
Collier-Macmillan Canada Ltd., Toronto, Ontario

Printed in the United States of America

This book is dedicated
to all the young people I have known and worked with
who are seeking to bring about change
in their society
and who can see very clearly
that changes must be made

# Contents

# *Foreword*

THE MOOD OF THIS BOOK makes it a must for all Americans. The mood reveals the depth of the anguish and anger in the Black community. I hope White America understands the mood. If we do, then we will know that tear gas and armed might are no answers to our problems.

This book has harsh words for almost every white man alive. The story, of course, is the accumulated grievances of the Blacks going back at least three centuries. It is a sad chronicle and one which those of us working in the vineyard —both White and Black—know only too well. There are Whites—yes, Whites in America—who are as passionate as any Blacks for creating a society of equal opportunities, not only equal civil rights for all. Those of us who made our way through high school, college, and law school know what difficulties the Black encounters along the road of education.

The praise of the Black Muslims is, I think, understandable as they have high personal standards. But the carry-over to the Moslem world in general gives one the creeps. For the greatest slave dealers in the world were Arabs; and many of the four million slaves held in bondage in 1969 are in Moslem lands. Come with me and I can

9

introduce you to the modern Middle East slave broker, more suave than Simon Legree, but engaged in the same dastardly business. The examples could be multiplied. But what I have said in criticism is in a sense largely irrelevant. For, as I said, the important thing is not the accuracy of the book but the mood.

Martin Luther King, Jr., was right in detecting a racist element in the ill-starred Vietnam venture. Racial prejudice —against Yellows, Browns, and Blacks—is deep-seated here; and it probably has its fiercest component in regard to the Yellow Peril. The Churchillian tradition of the West gets up a powerful head of steam when it comes to the Yellows, Browns, and Blacks on the move. I do not discount the destructive power of any of them. But I am so confident of the imaginative resources of the Chinese as to feel confident that the twenty-first century will belong to them.

I feel very deeply one truth articulated in this present book—that America will never be able to assert any moral leadership in the world until and unless we bury racism once and for all. When that happens, there will be a magical transformation.

Another arresting part of the book deals with the Constitution. Minorities today think of the Constitution as their great Magna Carta. Yet in the beginning slavery was safely ensconced in it—from which fact comes the book's title. And the fugitive slave laws had constitutional sanction. Moreover, the Supreme Court by a divided vote in the *Dred Scott* case deprived Congress of any effective power to do anything about the spread of slavery.

That constitutional crisis was resolved by the Civil War; and the Thirteenth, Fourteenth, and Fifteenth amendments were adopted to abolish slavery and admit the Blacks into first-class citizenship. The story of the halting legal victories won by the Blacks in the courts makes depressing reading.

The sad truth is that the legal talents of the time and the popular attitudes were behind other causes. The corporation —bent on exploiting American resources—was the beneficiary both of the Due Process clause and of the Equal Protection clause of the Fourteenth Amendment before the Blacks. The legal victories won by the Blacks were mostly grudging ones; and the "separate but equal" doctrine approved by the Supreme Court in 1896 sanctified the vicious Black Codes which held the Blacks in a tight vise. It took two generations of legal battles and the education and training of a Black elite among the lawyers to get rid of that stigma of segregation.

Moreover, the victory in the *Brown* case did not mark a revolutionary change in practice. Proponents of a segregated way of life fought the application of the case precinct by precinct, town by town, county by county. They were able to use that strategy because the federal courts are restricted to decisions of "cases" or "controversies." Johnny Jones may in time win his case. But Sam Smith, in like circumstances, may have to bring a brand-new law suit. Administrative agencies can order desegregation in all dining cars, passenger coaches and the like on and after a certain date. But the judicial power, as construed, does not extend as far. Victories (or defeats, as the case may be) turn on case after case after case. That means that much time, energy, and money must be spent in pursuit of civil rights. Congress, of course, can enforce the Civil War amendments by legislation; and at times it has provided comprehensive remedies.

The moral is that reliance on the courts is slow and exhausting, that political action is the better remedy. This book gives the reasons why that is true.

A man or a race caught in a pot of glue uses desperate efforts to escape. He does not listen patiently to those who expound his First Amendment rights and his right to vote, explaining that they provide an escape route. For those rights in practical operation have proved futile in the past and often promise only to imprison a minority in a useless constitutional ceremony. Dissent, debate, dialogue—these become empty words.

At the same time the violence and the other aspects of guerrilla warfare have no real place in our technological society. Our plants can be run only by trained men and women; we can keep abreast of world competition only by research and development; we can keep modern only by imaginative planning.

The truth of the matter is that whether Black or White, the only competent persons to run our technological society must be highly educated. The Black has suffered greatly by reason of an inferior education. The Black deserves as high a place in our technological society as anyone. He can get there only through education. Burning a ghetto expresses his mood but it does not advance the cause of education.

At the other end of the spectrum are perhaps 80 or 90 per cent of the people—Black and White, who will always be as unsuited for these managerial jobs as they are for brain surgery. What about them?

The truth is that we are facing an age of disemployment, not unemployment—more and more people being put out of work by the machine. The private sector in the years ahead cannot possibly take care of our employment needs.

Welfare is not the answer. For what kind of country would we have if unemployed or disemployed Blacks and Whites had no jobs but only relief? Man needs work if he is to stay healthy. If in the days ahead there is to be work for everyone—Black and White alike—it must be found in the public sector.

When it comes to domestic affairs, the great debates of 1968 are about minuscule issues. We need a public sector of employment; we need an abolition of the welfare system (except for the aged and infirm); we need the best brains of Blacks and Whites working on those blueprints.

Unhappily, little if anything of the kind is being done. We talk the old, outdated clichés, when they no longer have relevancy—as little relevancy as violence in educating people for the top managerial jobs or in drafting blueprints for full employment through both the private and public sector.

Progress in making this nation a multiracial community dedicated to equal justice and equal opportunities for all entails tremendous undertakings. The book points out how it is that the legal profession has represented the affluent society, not the underprivileged and the poor. Many of our laws have a built-in bias against the poor who have had few to represent them and make articulate their complaints. That is being changed. Neighborhood Legal Services under OEO has many offices manned with lawyers who now are protecting the poor, both Black and White. The Blacks are accepting the challenge of legal education and making their appearance before agencies and courts in increasing numbers. The bias of the bench in some areas, like the bias of the bar associations, is against minority groups. But that too is changing; and the change can be dramatic and conclusive if we all insist that legal education be opened freely to the Blacks and that they be vigorously promoted for all the honors which the law offers, whether it be prosecutor or judge.

This is important, for racism is defeated not by laws enacted but by laws equally enforced and administered by sturdy men and women.

WILLIAM O. DOUGLAS

# Introduction

MY PRIMARY CONCERN is not with saving white America; I am concerned with liberating Black America. That is what compels me to write this book. It attempts to outline the contours of what must be done, and, more importantly, it suggests that we possess the instruments to do it. It may be that this book should have been written ten years ago—or in 1954, or in 1865, or in 1787. It may be too late now to reverse the great tides of racism and the sickening righteousness that has cloaked those forces.

White America today simply does not understand what is happening. And worse, it still assumes that everyone else lives as it does, with fine homes, healthy children, good schools, protected by law. Its ideals and historical myths all support these illusions. I doubt whether white thinking has seriously progressed beyond the missionary mentality of the eighteenth-century European racists who founded this nation: the Black heathens had to be "civilized." And what a lesson in civility it was! White America chooses property over Black life. I doubt that we have yet shunned those primitive deceptions.

But what is more important, I cannot detect a willingness

among this nation's leaders to undertake the drastic reversals in their thinking required to help Blacks attain their deserved Black Power, which would be the same thing as helping their fellow whites effect the survival of this country. And there have been dramatic signals given—nonviolent protests, violent protests, assassinations, lynchings, beatings, voices from the moderates through younger revolutionaries who speak louder still—but these have gone unheeded.

Will white America continue to deny itself its own liberation? Will it continue to delude itself with speechmaking and legislation, believing all the time that a few more dollars in paternalistic poverty programs and a few more Black cops pounding the ghetto beat will give us a new life? Will it continue to believe that Black Power is separatism in the worst devisive way?

The survival of white America and the liberation of Black America are irredeemably linked. The three themes suggested in these pages are not separate approaches; racism and international capitalism, the effective utilization of the Declaration of Independence and the Constitution of the United States, and the development of Black Nationhood in this country are all obviously related.

Considering the international aspects of racism and capitalism, the United States is fortunately blessed with two documents that transcend racist attitudes and methods. The spirit of the Declaration—"all men are created equal"—and the goals of the Constitution—the Thirteenth and Fourteenth amendments—provide the federal government and the American people with all the political justification, legal authorization, moral impetus, and historical basis required to liberate the Blacks in this country. The full and immediate use of these two documents—they can be seen as one—is the one way to be militant without hating. I describe in Chapter 2 the reasons why we must employ it. This chapter provides a historical outline of the role of the Supreme Court in our history by highlighting certain significant cases.

*But let me make one point very clear: this "double document" must be used to help Blacks attain not only civil rights and civil liberties but also human rights and human liberties.*

The Constitution and the Declaration of Independence are the heart of this nation's social, legal, and political spirit; and it is to the heart that we must return, or the whole body will sicken and die. Nothing less will be satisfactory.

I have been a constitutional lawyer since 1952. Practicing law in the South, I have witnessed the deliberate destruction of constitutional freedoms and the perversion of the American legal system. And yet, at the same time, I have become convinced that the "double document" (the Constitution and the Declaration of Independence) does indeed provide the opportunity for great and fundamental social change in this country.

It is one thing to say that the instruments for attacking *de facto* slavery exist; it is entirely another matter that they will indeed be used. If massive, violent, destructive Black-white confrontations are still to be avoided, these instruments must be used. Not tomorrow but today.

While I have presented in this book no cure-all program or panacea, I do believe that the ideas suggested herein can and must be a beginning. I am not sanguine about the future, but at least it can never be said that "we didn't know."

FLOYD McKISSICK

# PART 1

# *What Is Happening Now?*

*Representatives and direct Taxes shall be apportioned among the several States which may be included within this Union, according to their respective Numbers, which shall be determined by adding to the whole Number of free Persons, including those bound to Service for a Term of Years, and excluding Indians not taxed, three fifths of all other Persons . . .*

Constitution of the United States
Article 1, Section 2(C)

## We're in the Same Boat Brother

We're in the same boat brother,
We're in the same boat brother,
And if you shake one end, you gonna rock the other.
It's the same boat brother.

The Lord looked down from his holy place
Said Lawd de me, what a sea of space,
What a spot to launch the human race.
So he built him a boat for a mixed-up crew,
With eyes of Black and Brown and Blue.
So that's how's come that you and I
Got just one world and just one sky.

We're in the same boat brother,
We're in the same boat brother,
And if you shake one end, you gonna rock the other.
It's the same boat brother.

Through storm and grief,
Hit many a rock and many a reef,
What keep them going was a great belief.
That the Human race was a special freight
So they had to learn to navigate.
If they didn't want to be in Jonah's shoes,
Better be mated on this here cruise.—Why—

We're in the same boat brother,
We're in the same boat brother,
And if you shake one end, you gonna rock the other.
It's the same boat brother.

So the boiler blew, somewhere in Spain,
All the kettle was smashed and 40 cranes.
Steam boat out from the Oregon Main.
Oh, it took some time for the crew to learn
What is bad for the bow ain't good for the stern.
If a fire took place in China today,
Pearl Harbor just gonna blaze away.

We're in the same boat brother,
We're in the same boat brother,
And if you shake one end, you gonna rock the other.
It's the same boat brother.

—Hudie Leadbelly

THE INEVITABLE is happening. History is catching up with America. For the first time since the American system of racism, exploitation, and oppression was developed, it is seriously being threatened.

The Man has been warned. As in the case of other world civilizations, there have been signs of impending doom. Rome, Carthage, Athens—all highly developed civilizations —ignored the warnings of history, only to fall from power and then to decay.

Vietnam and Detroit, Cuba and Watts, Cambodia and Newark, all sound the cry that warns America to change —or be destroyed.

But it does not appear that America or the capitalist system that America dominates has the ability to change. Capitalism is a system that preaches the maintenance of the status quo at all costs. It is a system dependent for its very existence upon the rigid standards of class and caste—no matter how vehemently its proponents profess equality of man.

The capitalist system by nature has demanded cheap labor upon which to feed. It has required an inferior, dependent people to create the wealth that is reinvested for the benefit of the few.

In most of the world, particularly Latin America, Africa, and Asia, cheap labor is still very much a necessity for the feudal economies still dependent upon the United States. However, within the boundaries of the United States, automation has made such a labor force all but obsolete.

In the time that automation has been taking over America, few steps have been taken for the retraining and education of the displaced Black People who historically have provided cheap labor. No steps have been taken to facilitate the redistribution of the nation's wealth.

The poor have been ignored. They have been isolated from the rest of the society—without adequate nourishment, medical services, education, or housing. Lacking these tools, they have been ill equipped to compete in this complex society. They have been trapped in the bonds of their own poverty.

White America has refused to accept its responsibilities to the Black poor—the products of a brutal system of slavery, blocked every step of the way from participating in the economy, prevented even from being "homesteaders," left landless, moneyless, and uneducated after the Civil War. At no time did America offer opportunity to the Black masses; at no time did the Black population receive the chances offered every other group of immigrants—the Irish, the Italians, the Jews, the Poles.

In America caste is defined by color, class by economic status. A man's color, if it is Black, is most frequently used as a means of enforcing economic limitations. It is used as a visible tool of oppression. Morality is a nonexistent force in America. Religion has deteriorated to the point where it merely reinforces the system. Churches have become a haven for the oppressor and a shield for his crimes.

In the same short speech, the President of the United States announced that federal paratroopers had been sent to Detroit and called for a national day of prayer. That speech symbolized for many American Black People the hypocrisy and cruelty of the present system and its leaders.

Religion can be valid only when it is addressed to the needs of the people—not to the whims of the masters. No valid religion can uphold a system that subjugates and exploits more than one-half of the world's population. Yet the policies of every major religious institution, Protestant, Catholic, and Jewish, are in some way affected by what is economically expedient. This expediency has led religious institutions into many secular fields of endeavor, such as real-estate speculation and the manufacture of such miscellaneous items as wines and jellies—all tax-exempt capitalist enterprises.

These commitments have served to unite further the religious community with the business community, consequently obscuring the supposed primary moral commitments of the church. (Even the Pope of the Roman Catholic Church is subject to political and secular pressures. Capitulation to such pressure was evident in the disregard of the heir apparent to Cardinal Spellman of New York in the appointing of the Cardinal's successor. In his place the present Archbishop of New York, Terence Cooke, a comparatively conservative prelate, was appointed.)

Ironically, that which has been done, said, and taught by American religious leaders in their attempts to keep their churches solvent and viable is that which has cost the church its right to moral leadership and every vestige of clerical independence—creating a vacuum that has never been filled and providing unprincipled politicians with a chance to exploit the vacuum.

The result of this moral irresponsibility has been a racist system, reinforced by many of its religious institutions and beliefs. And the result of this system has been a white man without morality. Any man who really believes in his own superiority cannot deal morally with those he considers inferior. It is not possible for a racist white man to judge a crime committed against Blacks as he would judge one committed against whites—and since the white man controls the administration of justice, Black Men cannot possibly be treated with fairness.

In the minds of whites, distinctions exist even between genocides. World-wide horror greeted the revelations of Nazi Germany's extermination of innocent Jews. Little attention was paid to the systematic mutilation and extermination of Congolese by the Belgians. White Europeans and Americans seemed unmoved by pictures and reports of Black Congolese by the thousands having their hands cut off as punishment for not working fast enough. They were indifferent to the wanton murders of hundreds of thousands of Blacks, but they responded with indignation and alarm when white missionaries lost their lives.

The duplicity of standards is clear. White Americans are dismayed by the mass murder of whites by other whites, as indicated by their bitter reaction to the slaughter of Jews by the Nazis. They are indifferent to the mass murder of colored people by other colored people, even when such murders are financed and inspired by white foreigners. In Indonesia approximately four million nonwhite people died as a result of mass executions by a regime supported by the American CIA. White Americans tacitly condone the mass murder of nonwhite people by whites—as in the Congo, Algeria, Vietnam, India, South Africa, Rhodesia, and Kenya. Their acceptance of the murder and torture of nonwhites by whites is clearly established historically in their own land. It is in America that the Indian was exterminated and that the lives of Blacks were made cheap. But the horror and outrage of white Americans is reserved for the few occasions when whites are killed by Blacks.

The inconsistencies and cruelties of America make it unlikely for the Black Man to be reconciled with the system. When a system minimizes the worth of a Black life, it is not likely that a Black Man who is truly free will elect to continue that kind of degradation.

The English—once the greatest colonialist power in the world—had the good sense to withdraw from Kenya when the Mau Mau relayed the message that they were no longer welcome.

Not America. Black People in Harlem, Watts, Detroit, Newark, Tampa, Miami, Syracuse, Plainfield, and dozens of other American cities have given the message that the white cops, white storekeepers, and white national guardsmen are not welcome. But white America has had neither the grace nor the foresight to withdraw.

America's mayors and governors have shown an amazing lack of perception and astounding shortsightedness. White Americans seem to feel that rebellions born of anger and oppression can be squelched by an Anti-Riot Bill—a bill that addresses itself not to the causes of the rebellions but to restricting the free speech and travel of Black leaders. But with each Black Man who is jailed or killed in the quest for his freedom, another revolutionary hero is created. For each Black leader who is silenced, another Black Man, even more militant, will take his place. For each atrocity committed against Black People, revolutionary zeal increases and the task of policing the ghetto becomes more costly—and more dangerous.

While Black Men in America fight for their freedom, all over the world oppressed people—almost always nonwhites —are rising up to demand that changes be made. The list of nations established in the last decade as a direct or indirect consequence of violence is staggering.

Ghana, Mali, Senegal, Algiers, Tanzania, Zanzibar, Vietnam, Korea, China, Chad, Kenya, Malawi, Botswanaland, Ivory Coast, Cuba—not all of these revolutions have been successful. None have been completed. But this is only the beginning. Revolutionary movements in Africa, Asia, and Latin America, as well as in northern ghettos, challenge the system.

The cheap-labor market is awakening. The people who

comprise that market are realizing that their problems are not only local, regional, or even national in dimension. Oppressed people in the colonies and former colonies of England, Belgium, Portugal, France, Holland—and the oppressed Black People of America—realize their common destinies. Colored and Black People know that racism and capitalism are so entwined as to be inseparable. And they know that they are the victims.

On a world-wide basis, Black and colored people are numerically superior. The Man has refused to recognize openly that we cannot stay docile—that we have an innate capacity at least equal to his own. Perhaps, if only subconsciously, The Man now recognizes this—or he would not be running scared; he would not be maintaining such feverish holding actions in so many parts of the world.

In Latin America and in Africa and Asia, American troops and American dollars support the status quo. In Cuba, the United States first supported the Batista dictatorship since it was advantageous for American business interests. Only when it became apparent that Castro could not be stopped short of armed United States intervention did this country accept his regime. When the new revolutionary regime nationalized American industry and dared to seek economic independence, America responded by imposing economic sanctions against the tiny country. Only when Cuba sought to make its revolution meaningful by diversifying its one crop economy—once totally dependent on sugarcane products—did the American government and press convey belated horror at the political executions of the Castro regime.

It should be remembered that for a short while after Castro took power, he seemed to have the approval of the American people. He was depicted in the press as a romantic figure—a bearded, latter-day Robin Hood. The press acknowledged, somewhat belatedly, that Batista had been a cruel and oppressive dictator; Castro was hailed as a needed change.

But when Castro began to move for change by nationalizing American industry, the tone of the American press altered drastically. Suddenly there was sensationalized coverage of political executions by the Castro regime. Castro was depicted as a murderer and thief, more cruel and oppressive than his predecessor, even though the executions were of men who had tortured and murdered innocent Cubans for years.

The United States became so committed to Castro's overthrow and so anxious to reclaim the nationalized industries that the CIA in 1961 armed a group of anti-Castro Cuban refugees to attack Cuba, precipitating the disaster of the Bay of Pigs. It is also significant that the United States willingly provides a haven for those refugees who had been associated with Batista and who were from the privileged class prior to the revolution. The hatred of Castro by these refugees seems to stem from the fact that the new regime enforced more social and economic equality than had ever before existed.

Castro was forced to turn to Russia for help and has had to rely on Communist countries for Cuba's foreign economic support. Almost invariably, people fighting for independence and freedom in these underdeveloped nations must turn to the Communist countries for aid. Freedom fighters usually need resources from outside countries. Their fight would not be necessary if they were allowed to share in the wealth of their own lands. The practice of seeking foreign assistance for domestic revolutions is well established historically. The French turned to Italy and Austria to aid their revolution, and, more significantly, the American colonists received aid from the French in their war for independence from England. Individual nations that have turned to Communist regimes for assistance—often because there was nowhere else to turn—have been labeled "Communist" by our State Department. Once having labeled the rebels Communist, our government feels free to intervene on behalf of the ruling class, the oppressive few who control the economies of their native lands.

It is often these few—the ruling elite—who prevent the diversification and independence of their country's economy. They are the only ones who gain by keeping the economy dependent upon the United States, for it is not expensive for the United States to keep these greedy men quiet, particularly when compared to the toll that economic justice for the populations of these nations would impose. It would mean that American industries—industries that have lived off the fat of other lands, that have exploited other people as cheap labor—would be nationalized. It would mean that these countries would be free to trade with whom they choose; sometimes it would be the United States, sometimes it would be Russia, sometimes Communist China. Economic justice would force the United States to alter its own economy radically—to change those features of capitalism that make it dependent upon these poor countries and these poor populations for a favorable balance of trade.

Such nations as England, France, and Belgium have been forced to relinquish their colonies. The process of dispossessing these colonialists was long, bloody, painful, and difficult. If America persists in its present policies, the wars to dispossess Uncle Sam will be even longer, bloodier, more painful, and more difficult than their predecessors. But the issues will not be as strikingly clear.

The United States has never been as honest in its intentions as its predecessors. The French had the honesty in 1883 to declare Vietnam, then Indo-China, a French protectorate, subject to French colonial rule. Similar policies were executed by the English in such places as Kenya and by the

Belgians in the Congo. America has rarely followed suit—at least not openly. Of course, it should be noted that it was under policies of expansionism very similar to the French and English that the United States became the power it is today. It was only by the subjugation of Indians and annexation of the Indians' homelands that America became a land of fifty states. It was by policies almost identical to those of the Europeans that the United States became the colonial governor of such places as the U.S. Virgin Islands and Puerto Rico.

Nevertheless, it is true that American relations with the Latin American and South American countries have not been as clearly defined or as honest as the relations of European imperialists to Africa and Asia. For instance, when England was colonial governor of Kenya, the Mau Mau rebellion had a certain legitimacy, recognized even by some western nations. This legitimacy was evident in the fact that Kenya was, in fact, occupied and governed by a foreign nation. The same legitimacy existed for the Algerians who rebelled against French colonial rule.

America has developed alternate means for remaining a colonial power. In Latin America, the United States has made a practice of directly taking over the economies (this economic control all but guaranteeing political control) rather than officially moving in itself. The rulers of the Latin American regimes are free to use torture and murder—financed by the Americans—to keep the peasant populations in their places. American troops are sent in, as in the case of Santo Domingo, on the pretense of saving "democracy" and "free enterprise" (i.e., the ruler who is directly responsible to us).

This comparative sophistication has made the United States a most formidable oppressor—a phantom super power difficult to attack directly. American representatives

31

to these countries are usually sent by such industries as United Fruit Company, Standard Oil, or Coca-Cola, and Americans rarely occupy the land with troops.

In Vietnam, of course, the situation has been somewhat different. The French were the original occupiers, the United States offering first tacit support and, as early as 1950, direct military aid to the French colonialists.

In 1954, Secretary of State John Foster Dulles told the Overseas Press Club: "The United States has shown in many ways its sympathy for the gallant struggle being waged in Indo-China by French forces and those of the Associated States. Congress has enabled us to provide material aid to the established governments and their peoples."

It was after the total French defeat at Dienbienphu that America openly took over for the French. Once again America applied the policy of deceit. Americans did not occupy Vietnam in the same forthright manner as the French; gradually the United States escalated its "aid" to the corrupt ruling regime.

After sending "observers," we sent "technical advisers"; after "technical advisers," we sent troops. The American government does not even identify its troops as colonialists —our representatives tell the world that these troops were invited by the Diem regime (a mere formality, in the tradition of American foreign policy). And once again the world is expected to believe that we are, in fact, fighting another "war against Communism."

Americans do, however, seem to lack the sensitivity of their French brothers, who at least have demonstrated their ability to make a hasty retreat when beaten—and to withdraw with a maximum of grace when defeated. Dienbienphu taught the French to get out of Vietnam. The United States hasn't learned even that much.

The Vietnamese fought valiantly to drive the French from

their land only to be cursed with a bigger, more powerful, and greedier foe—the United States of America. Once again it has been shown that it is not possible to eliminate oppression simply by removing the immediate oppressor. The entire system must be revamped.

If the American system is sufficiently altered to end its dependence on subjugated economies, whether these changes come by full-scale violent revolution or by some miracle of peaceful revolution, the system will have become a "socialist democracy." Even if a basic minimum change was made (e.g., establishing a guaranteed annual income for every American or the abolition of the wage and welfare systems), the amount of possible exploitation would be limited and capitalism restricted. If these changes were sufficient to provide every American with a share of the economy, capitalism will not only have been restricted, but redesigned.

If large sections of the present economy were transferred to the Black Community and if all the American poor were given a stake in capitalism, the situation at home would be greatly improved, but it would not change in the rest of the world. But although such a "solution" would be inadequate, it would be worth the effort to establish if only to alleviate the suffering of the American poor and the American Black —to end the oppression of a people who have suffered on these shores for hundreds of years.

Until at least these minimal changes occur, American Black People face daily degradations. They face discrimination in all aspects of their lives. Black People are exploited economically, politically, psychologically, and culturally. Their family lives are undermined by a system that castrates Black Men and often prevents them from being effective heads of their families. Their religious lives are cheapened by a system that utilizes theology as a weapon.

Although Black People have not been allowed to integrate into American life, they are, nevertheless, strategically located: Black People live in every major city, near every major industrial complex in America.

This pattern developed from an unplanned, unorganized migration of southern Blacks who sought jobs in the northern industrial areas. The treatment these people received in the North was as degrading and obscene as they had received in Dixie.

They were generally untrained and could find only menial employment. When minor recessions afflicted the economy, Black People suffered acutely. They were forced to live in the least appealing and least comfortable areas of the city —in places where the noise and dirt of industry was the greatest—where white people didn't want to live. Black People living in these urban areas are the closest, physically, to luxury. They are domestics in the homes of the rich, laborers in the factories of the powerful.

When the anger of the Black Man spills into the streets in Detroit and Newark, America's production centers are threatened. As the Black Man becomes more sophisticated in his revolution, America will be unable to deal with his fury.

If America is to avoid this fury, piecemeal solutions will not be adequate. A few more jobs for middle-class Negroes and a few more Black cops pounding beats in the ghettos will not be the answer. The wealth of America will have to be redistributed among the people—the affluence of America will have to include the Black population.

The Office of Economic Opportunity (laughingly called the "War on Poverty"), the Civil Rights Bills, the Voters

Rights Bill—all are examples of piecemeal solutions to complex problems—all pitifully inadequate and consequently failing. Even if unemployment were eliminated tomorrow, the system would not be saved. For even full employment would not guarantee the working man his full share. Within thirty-six hours after the first day in a week of national full employment, about 68 percent of the money would be back in the hands of the capitalists—in the form of rent, food bills, and other essentials.

Whites frequently allude to South America as an example of integration at work. But we have seen that the United States controls the economies of South America and keeps those countries dependent. Poverty, disease, and suffering are common in Latin and South America, particularly among the darker populations.

In any case, the history of South America is significantly different from our own. The slavery in the United States was probably the most oppressive form of slavery the world has ever seen. In every other slaveholding culture, the slave had a few basic rights: he was always recognized as a human being—however unfortunate or servile.

In America the slave was chattel. He was literally the property of his master. The white master had absolute control over the life and death of his slaves; there was no effective court of appeals, no hope for justice.

Very little of the original African culture was permitted to survive in this country. Slaves were not allowed to converse in their native tongues and were usually separated from members of their families and tribal groups in order to prevent communication and possible conspiracy. The Africans were not allowed to practice their own religions or worship their own gods. They were forced to adopt Christianity.

Nevertheless, some of their culture survived or was modified to meet their new needs. "Spirituals," the hymns of the slaves—the first freedom songs—became part of America's heritage. These songs were often used by the slaves as a coded form of communication. For instance, a popular slave song, "Follow the Drinking Gourd," was used by Black members of the Underground Railroad to tell their fellow slaves the way north. (The drinking gourd referred to the north-pointing stellar constellation, the Big Dipper.)

The Emancipation Proclamation attempted to free the slaves, but no substantial changes have occurred in the system since that historic document was written. Since the end of the Civil War, America has made serious mistakes, miscalculations that are having grave consequences.

One of the most serious mistakes was the failure of America to provide forty acres and a mule to every freed slave, as was promised by the military when Black troops were needed by the Union to win the Civil War. There were white people as well as Black in 1860 who recognized that the only feasible way to deal with the vast poverty of the freed slave was to provide a program of massive economic aid. But the landed interests and even the poor whites objected to such a notion, and the slaves were left to their own devices —unprotected and without resources. The freed Black Men could not even move westward to claim rights as homesteaders—such land was reserved for "whites only."

By not providing economic opportunity for the former slaves, America missed the one chance to absorb Black People into the economic system. By developing Black capitalists at an early date, capitalism could have bought a great deal of time with a comparatively small investment.

Another error was the failure of the government to enforce the United States Supreme Court decision of *Brown* v. *the Board of Education* in 1954, which negated the previous doctrine of "separate but equal." The hope of Black People for decent education was dashed and many became hope-lessly disillusioned.

The passage of the Voters Rights Bill of 1965 provided the government with another tool that could have brought Black political power to the South as well as the North. At the time that bill was passed, civil-rights organizations had hundreds of volunteers ready to assist federal registrars —but only a few registrars ever came.

Since the political decision not to send those registrars south, not to enforce the law of the land, was made, only minimal benefits to Black southerners resulted from the Voters Rights Bill. In a few southern counties, Black regis-tration was increased enough through the tireless efforts of a few civil-rights workers to allow the election of a few Black sheriffs, such as Sheriff Lucius Amerson of Tuskegee County, Alabama.

But the gains were tiny in comparison to what this bill could have accomplished had there been a true commitment by those in power. And the result of the impotence of this potentially important legislation has been that many more Black People who had hoped there was a national con-science realized there was no such thing.

America also failed to understand the significance of the March on Washington in August of 1963. With one last plaintive cry, hundreds of thousands of Americans—white as well as Black—descended upon the nation's capital to dramatize their needs. They were ignored.

Although few realized it at the time—for the tone of that march was one of hope and optimism—much of the idealism and romanticism of the Civil Rights Movement died that day. For that demonstration culminated years of suffering and toil—and when that cry went unheeded, Black America began a revolution.

America had many opportunities to demonstrate good faith—many chances to prove good intentions. And each opportunity, each chance, was ignored—and opportunities are becoming scarcer every day.

Instead of constructively responding to those few remaining opportunities, the Congress of the United States has compounded the difficulty by making bad laws—laws directly in conflict with the letter as well as the intent of the Constitution.

Instead Congress passes anti-riot bills worked so vaguely as to be dangerous. An example is this passage from the 1968 Civil Rights Act (italics added):

(2) Whoever moves or travels in interstate or foreign commerce or uses any facility, instrumentality, or means of communication, transportation, or travel in interstate or foreign commerce, with intent to (a) incite, promote, encourage, or participate in, or facilitate the incitement, promotion, encouragement, or commission of a riot; or (b) obstruct, impede, or interfere with any fireman or law enforcement officer engaged in the performance of his official duties incident to and during the commisson of any riot—

Shall be fined not more than $10,000 or imprisoned not more than five years, or both.

(b) As used in this section—

(1) The term "riot" means any disturbance of the peace in any State or the District of Columbia, by *three or more persons* which results in unlawful acts of violence or depredations against persons or property *or threats* of the commission of such unlawful acts of violence or depredation *by three or more persons* who have the ability to perform the acts so threatened.

(2) The term "fireman" means any member of a fire department (including a volunteer fire department of any

State, any political subdivision of a State, or the District of Columbia . . .

Such a law could be invoked against any man questioning the status quo. For where does the legitimate statement of grievances end and "incitement to riot" begin? Surely if the answer to that question is left to the white law-enforcement officials, Black Men will not be able to exercise their right to free speech, their right to travel freely, or even their right to free assembly.

At the present rate of progress, it would take hundreds, possibly thousands, of years to make integration a reality. Yet integration is that for which white America would have us strive. Even the Report of the President's Commission on Civil Disorders, which is notable for its recognition of white racism as a cause of racial strife, urges the retention of integration as a goal.

Yet it is clear that Wall Street—the economic center of Western civilization—is not integrated. It is clear that the diamond markets and other world-power bases are still controlled by whites. And it is clear that the United States is actively working to maintain this situation. Chase Manhattan and First National City banks, along with many other large American investors in the South African economy, provide the economic base that allows the white South African minority to retain control.

It took years for America to reach this crossroad. It took decades for the wealth of the world to be concentrated in the hands of the few. And it took years of toil by poor people —years of slavery—to develop the momentum of capitalism.

America's economy in the days following the American Revolution was primarily agrarian. The inevitable transition from agrarian economy to industrial economy was painful and bloody. The Civil War accomplished the transition. The plantation system was, for all practical purposes, ended, and America was becoming an industrial society.

After the Civil War the northern capitalists consolidated their fortunes. Ruthless tactics were utilized by the men who were to control America's economy. Andrew Carnegie, Jay Gould, Pierpont Morgan, John Rockefeller, and others made their fortunes through the shrewd investment of stocks and properties. These "robber-barons" made their fortunes by absorbing and destroying small businesses and small businessmen—they made their fortunes while other Americans toiled in their mills and sweatshops. By 1936 their control was so complete that the country was dominated by approximately sixty families, supported by a smaller, less powerful elite of ninety families.

These industrialist families have united (even intermarried) to perpetuate and consolidate their dominance. They control not only the economy but, as an outgrowth of their economic control, the destinies of the American people and most of the people of the world.

These are the people who can afford to give away millions of tax-free dollars annually—financing foundations and subsidizing private education. They do so to salve their guilt and sense of responsibility to the poor exploited by their corporations. They do so, in addition, to take advantage of tax loopholes that protect the mass of their wealth. They seem to feel that such philanthropy somehow absolves their sins and guarantees their moral right to their remaining millions.

By monopolizing the wealth and resources of the country, these families are probably the one group most responsible for the status quo. They are the one group—these so-called philanthropists—most responsible for denying Black People the rights of self-determination, the acquisition of power, and the control of their own communities.

This is true because they are the people with the material means to transfer power. They are the people with the influence to force other sectors of society to relinquish power. Yet they are the people who remain the most conservative, the most "respectable," and the most isolated from the problems of the Black population. They, more than anyone, are the enemy.

In order to retain economic control in a capitalist society, they have become the overseers of the economy—the cruel boss to those who must work to live and those who cannot work for lack of skills and opportunity. This powerful elite is the employer for 67 percent of the American labor market and, as such, supplies and controls the livelihoods of most working Americans.

Repressive economic policies vitally affect every institution. They affect the choice of a mayor of any town, sheriff of any county, president of any college, judge in any court. They affect who will exercise the rights of freedom of speech, freedom of the press, or, in fact, any constitutional right.

These basic freedoms are respected only when it is in the interest of the structure to do so. Excessive restrictions are placed on opponents to the war in Vietnam—particularly when the dissenters are members of the armed forces. The military seems to feel that the constitutional rights of soldiers are to be suspended from the day they are inducted until they are discharged. Dr. Howard Levy, a man whose conscience would not allow him to aid the war effort in Vietnam, was sentenced in June, 1967, to five years at hard labor. Dr. Levy's only crime was the refusal to train American servicemen in the skills of medicine—knowing that by doing so, he would be supporting the war effort and the slaughter of innocent Vietnamese.

Pfc. Howard Petrick, U.S. Army, was dishonorably discharged in March, 1968, for discussing his beliefs in socialism, racial equality, and his opposition to the war in Vietnam with his fellow soldiers—as well as for distributing socialist, anti-war, and anti-racist literature among his friends. (Freedom of the press becomes meaningless when there is no freedom to distribute literature: freedom to read is implied in the freedom to print.)

In the case of Pfc. Petrick, no allegations were made concerning the fulfillment of his responsibilities as a soldier. He simply sought to exercise his constitutional rights. Pfc. Petrick was fortunate in that he was ably defended and that he was allied with an organization that had a few resources, which they used for his legal defense and the preparation and distribution of literature and information to alert people about his case. He was fortunate in that committees and ad hoc groups were formed to publicize his plight. It is likely that if such activities had not been conducted, Petrick would have been summarily court-martialed and jailed. This is further evidence that without economic support, it is not possible to gain even minimal justice. Without the contributions of friends and colleagues, Pfc. Petrick could not have been heard. He would not have had a chance.

*Economic power is the first prerequisite for political power.* Unless the Black Man attains economic independence, any "political independence" will be an illusion. White intimidation and control, especially in the ghettos and the rural South, will continue as long as the Blacks are economically dependent. In Mississippi, for instance, white storeowners withhold credit from Blacks who register to vote, creating a loss of tools and fertilizer, food and commodities. The alternative is obvious: don't register to vote and the lifeblood of credit becomes available; don't register to vote and the white racists can perpetuate themselves in power. The fear expressed by many poor Blacks at the thought of registering to vote is fully understandable—it is the fear of not having enough to eat.

Economics and independence are invariably linked. In the example mentioned previously, the Cuban revolutionaries knew that control of Havana radio stations and government buildings meant little as long as United Fruit ruled the sugar plantations. Nationalization of industries, primarily American ones, was an attempt to achieve independence from the dominance of foreign influences, which had their own and not Cuban interests in mind. The motivation for the revolutionaries was a desire for freedom of choice, the freedom to initiate what they thought was necessary for their country and not what was needed to pacify large foreign companies.

The process of nationalization, of course, was painful to the United Fruit Company, which lost capital and profits. America's vehement protests of such take-overs are indicative of a recognition in this materialist society that economics and power are indeed related. Power expresses wealth; in America money doesn't talk—it screams. Black People can expect the same resistance. In their attempts to achieve Black ownership of business, Black participation in economic decisions, they are striving for nothing less than a Black "nationalization" of American wealth and the means for producing it.

Political power can be derived from a strong economic foundation, but it is doubtful whether the process works in reverse (corruption excluded). The election of Black mayors is important, but it is also important to realize that Black officials are at the mercy of wealthy white citizens who finance elections, fund creative civic-development programs, and possess the enormous prestige of wealth. It should be remembered that bank presidents are often more powerful than elected officials—they may not have as much "authority" but they often have more power. Since all politicians are dependent on others for support, we can see how much more difficult it is for Black potential political figures, who have no one of their own color to turn to.

A recent victim of this predicament is Percy Sutton, borough president of Manhattan, a Black moderate who announced his candidacy for the United States Senate in March of 1968. Sutton was forced to retract his decision shortly thereafter because he was unable to raise enough money for an effective political campaign. It seems that in New York—the financial capital of the western hemisphere and reputedly one of America's more "liberal" states—even a moderate Black candidate cannot gain sufficient financial support to make himself a serious contender. In such circumstances, it hardly seems likely that a more militant Black candidate would have a chance for success.

Even though Sutton sought office at a time when there was not one Black Democrat in the United States Senate —and only one Negro Republican, Ed Brooke of Massachusetts—the Democrats did not feel enough pressure to project a Black candidate and adequately fund his campaign. They did not feel put upon to exhibit their liberalism or progressiveness.

Sutton estimated that he would need at least half a million dollars to conduct a television and radio campaign. He would also need another million dollars to meet other campaign expenses. As the mass media gain increasing influence on American life, these costs will accelerate even further and politics will be, more than ever, a rich man's sport. Occasionally, of course, a poor man will be financed, but, of necessity, even men who are not wealthy themselves will have to represent the interests of the wealthy in order to retain financial support for their own candidacies. In New York, as in Mississippi, the poor are subject to intimidation. Even the token candidate who is not independently wealthy is becoming a rarity. At this time there are no poor men in the Senate. Even those who started with relatively little have become affluent since entering the Senate—hardly from their senatorial salaries.

Probably as a result of new sophistication on the part of politicians, a few Black Men are being allowed to enter the House and the Senate. But the rules are not the same for these Black legislators as for their white "colleagues." This was made obvious in the actions taken by the Senate and the House in the cases of Congressman Adam Clayton Powell, Black Democrat of New York, and Senator Thomas Dodd, white Democrat of Connecticut. Powell was summarily stripped of his seniority and expelled from the House, leaving his Harlem constituency unrepresented, for alleged misconduct far less serious than that of Dodd—who was merely censured. The Powell case provides an excellent example of the power of the courts. A single white judge, through the use of injunctive powers, contempt proceedings, and fines, stripped Powell of power conferred upon him by thousands of constituents.

Although most new Black congressmen have been elected from predominantly Black areas, it is ironic that the only Black senator since Reconstruction, Edward Brooke, is representing Massachusetts, a state in which a small minority of the voters are Black. Perhaps this is partially because white voters in such a state are psychologically less threatened by a Black representative. They know that their numerical superiority will enable them to control his actions. If he deviates from their wishes, he will not be re-elected. Meanwhile

Massachusetts residents congratulate themselves on their liberalism in electing a Negro to the Senate—and there is quite a distinction between a Negro and a Black Man, the Negro being an invention of American racist society—to the Senate. They do so even though poverty and racism allows the existence of Boston's Black ghetto—Roxbury—and even though their relatively small Black population is as oppressed as elsewhere.

America is a study of contradictions. But in Boston, as well as Harlem and Atlanta, racism is the dominant reality. It is racism that controls the electorate and the electoral process. It is racism that controls the actions of the judiciary and the legislature. Racism infects the policies of the United States—as well as other colonialist nations—in all dealings with racial minorities at home and abroad. Unless this is purged, all attempts at justice will be useless.

White America has mistreated and suppressed the Black population in America, antagonized and provoked the non-white populations of countries around the world.

If violent rebellion spreads into general revolution, it will be white America who will be the losers. For Black People have little to lose. Black People will be fighting for their humanity—white people will be fighting for their property and their lives.

If such revolution becomes reality, it will be better for Black Men than accepting degradation and oppression. It will be better than living in a land where we are despised, where we are mistreated and regarded as less than men. If it happens, white America will go down with us.

White America must apply its resources and ingenuity in solving the problems of our times. Only then can there be hope to avoid world-wide violence. The avenues of change exist, if only in theory. *The Constitution of the United States is the most vital and real of these avenues.*

Black People cannot wait for white America to act. For their own self-preservation, Black People must take steps to free themselves. If white America does not respond to peaceful protest, if it does not respond to limited rebellion, Black People will be forced to work for their liberation through violent revolution. There will be no other way.

If the entire burden for change is left to Black People, they will be forced to meet the challenge with violence, for they alone cannot apply the Constitution. Black People alone cannot peacefully alter the system. But they can destroy it. Perhaps the threat of this destruction will force the American people to seek justice.

# PART 2

# The Constitution and Social Change

## Constitution of the United States
### Amendment 13

Section 1. Neither slavery nor involuntary servitude, except as a punishment for crime whereof the party shall have been duly convicted, shall exist within the United States, or any place subject to their jurisdiction.

Section 2. Congress shall have power to enforce this article by appropriate legislation.

### Amendment 14

Section 1. All persons born or naturalized in the United States and subject to the jurisdiction thereof, are citizens of the United States and of the State wherein they reside. No State shall make or enforce any law which shall abridge the privileges or immunities of citizens of the United States; nor shall any State deprive any person of life, liberty, or property, without the due process of law; nor deny to any person within its jurisdiction the equal protection of the laws.

## I Wonder When I'll Get To Be Called a Man?

When I was born into this world, this what happened to me,
I was never called a man and now I'm fifty-three.
I wonder when! I wonder when!
I wonder when will I get to be called a man,
Do I have to wait till I get 93?

When Uncle Sam called me, I knowed I'd be called the real
  McCoy.
When I got in the Army, they just called me soldier boy.
I wonder when! I wonder when!
I wonder when will I get to be called a man,
Do I have to wait till I get 93?

When I got back from overseas, that night we had a ball.
Next day I met the old boss and he said boy get you some
  overalls.
I wonder when! I wonder when!
I wonder when will I get to be called a man,
Do I have to wait till I get 93?

I worked on Levy camps and extra gangs too.
Black Man's a boy, don't care what he can do.
I wonder when! I wonder when!
I wonder when will I get to be called a man,
Do I have to wait till I get 93?

They said I was uneducated, clothes was dirty and torn.
Now I got a little education, but I'm still a boy right on.
I wonder when! I wonder when!
I wonder when will I get to be called a man,
Do I have to wait till I get 93?

—Big Bill Broonzy

B LACK PEOPLE have survived three hundred years of slavery in America. They have survived a bloody Civil War in which they were the pawns of white men. Black Men have survived the Reconstruction and its brutal aftermath. They have survived the Industrial Revolution. And they have survived modern American racism.

The patterns of behavior between the races that were developed during the earliest days of physical enslavement still exist. Every Black-white relationship is in some way affected by the heritage of a master-slave and master-servant tradition. Black-white distrust, Black-white fear, and Black-white tensions are deep rooted and real.

If they are ever to be reconciled, all the great forces of American revolution must be marshaled to this end. The Declaration of Independence and the Constitution of the United States must be revitalized to include Black Men, for unfortunately the Constitution was not written with the Black Man in mind. It was written by white men, many of whom owned Black slaves. It was written to perpetuate and protect their way of life. It was written to institutionalize racism.

In theory, the Declaration of Independence and the Constitution of the United States provide the means by which to achieve a free nation. *If* they are extended to their full potential, they can become the basis for a new and nonracist society.

The Declaration of Independence is a separatist document. Through that document the thirteen original American colonies declared themselves separate and free from the British empire, separate from the British constitution, separate from British law. The Declaration of Independence was also a revolutionary document. It established the intent and determination of the colonists to fight for their independence by any means, to sacrifice lives, to shoot and kill, to use violence and force to protect their right of freedom.

We hold these truths to be self-evident, that all men are created equal, that they are endowed by their Creator with certain unalienable rights, that among these are life, liberty and the pursuit of happiness. That to secure these rights, governments are instituted among men, deriving their just powers from the consent of the governed, that whenever any form of government becomes destructive of these ends, it is the right of the people to alter or to abolish it, and to institute new government, laying its foundation on such principles and organizing its powers in such form, as to them shall seem most likely to effect their safety and happiness. Prudence, indeed, will dictate that governments long established should not be changed for light and transient causes; and accordingly all experience hath shown that mankind are more disposed to suffer, while evils are sufferable, than to right themselves by abolishing the forms to which they are accustomed. But when a long train of abuses and usurpations, pursuing invariably the same object evinces a design to reduce them under absolute despotism, it is their right, it is their duty, to throw off such government, and to provide new guards for their future security. . . .

With these words the Declaration of Independence recognizes the right of revolution to overthrow oppression. It establishes the duty and obligation of honorable men to challenge the status quo—when the status quo perpetuates evil and inequity.

The Declaration of Independence acknowledges that if a government is not responsive to the needs and desires of the people, such government is, in fact, illegal and must be brought down.

Whereas the Declaration of Independence articulated the ideology of the American revolution, the Constitution was written to establish a framework through which that ideology could be translated into reality. It was written to provide a basis for the legal structure of a new nation, to provide a means by which to defend the rights and liberties set forth earlier and to make them more explicit.

Although the Constitution was at best imperfect, it created an outline for the impartial administration of justice. Even though it was conceived and developed by racists, the guarantees incorporated, if extended to all men, could be the basis for a truly free society. Most of the ideas included in the Constitution are sound and still viable, for the Constitution is a brilliant document born of a valid revolution. *If interpreted justly, in full awareness of today's conditions, and if applied in a consistent fashion, the Constitution can be converted into a document of liberation for Black America.*

The severe limitation of the Constitution is that it was written by men incapable of including nonwhites in their concept of revolutionary justice and freedom. In view of the stated purposes of the American Revolution, white Americans should have no difficulty understanding the aspirations of Black Americans today, for they are the same aspirations once expressed by the American colonists. They are the same aspirations for which the American Revolution was fought.

Proper use of the Constitution can be a way to put the full power and resources of the national government into the drive to gain freedom—the drive to achieve Black Power. As Howard Zinn, in *SNCC: The New Abolitionists,* has pointed out, the Constitution provides every possible authorization needed to enforce the Thirteenth and Fourteenth amendments. The legal authority is present; the will is plainly lacking. The Constitution must be enforced—Black People will not and should not have to wait until white America realizes its own evil. The Constitution provides white America with a way for immediate and complete action; it does not presuppose that Blacks have to wait until America somehow undergoes massive self-education to exorcise itself of racism.

Indicative of the white American psyche is the section of the original Constitution that determines the representation and means of taxation for the state. According to Article 1, Section 2(C):

Representatives and direct Taxes shall be apportioned among the several States which may be included in this Union, according to their respective Numbers, which shall be determined by adding to the whole Number of free Persons, including those bound to Service for a Term of Years, and excluding Indians not taxed, three fifths of all other persons.

"All other persons" meant Black People. Taken in context, its implications are staggering. It meant that the slave was considered less than human, a bit more than an animal, perhaps, but less than human. If you were Black, you were only three-fifths of a man in the eyes of Alexander Hamilton, Benjamin Franklin, Roger Sherman, Charles Pickney, James Madison, John Blair, Robert Morris, and the other witnesses in Philadelphia. The Black Man in America has had to live with this stigma of inferiority all his life—a stigma imposed upon him by men who assumed the prerogative of bargaining with his life and destiny.

We must look beyond the immediate reasons why this clause was included in the Constitution—whether it was for acceptance by southern states, whether it was to guarantee the continuation of the plantation economy, or for representation in the new Congress. These are unimportant to the

Black Man. Racism had been written into the Constitution. This was the first time in recorded history that such an attitude was officially recognized and sanctioned by a national government.

The hypocrisy of the white slaveholders, evidenced in the Declaration of Independence, was not repeated in the writing of the Constitution; at last true feelings came out. As was written in No. 54 of *The Federalist* (generally attributed to James Madison), "The Federal Constitution, therefore, decides with great propriety on the case of our slaves, when it views them in the mixed character of persons and of property. This is in fact their true character."

So protective of the institution of slavery were America's Founding Fathers that they took care to include in Article 4, Section 2(C):

No Person held to Service or Labour in one State, under the laws thereof, escaping into another, shall, in Consequence of any Law or Regulation therein, be discharged from such Service or Labour, but shall be delivered up on Claim of the Party to whom such Service or Labour may be due.

This meant that a slave or a freedman, upon a white man's "claim," could be returned to bondage. There was no rest or hope for the fugitive slave. Nowhere in the "land of the free" was there a place where a Black Man could walk tall, without fear of re-enslavement or death.

There was some opposition to the expansion of slavery within the colonies. It is likely that a good deal of the opposition was based on fear by whites of slave insurrection, not egalitarian principles. Article 1, Section 9(A) of the Constitution reads:

The Migration or Importation of such Persons as any of the States now existing shall think proper to admit, shall not be prohibited by the Congress prior to the Year one thousand eight hundred and eight, but a tax or duty may be imposed on such Importation, not exceeding ten dollars for each Person.

That section was included in order to buy time—to forestall the opposition to slavery and to make the process of importing slaves more costly, though certainly not contraband.

Thomas Jefferson and his fellow authors apparently did realize the cruel hypocrisy of admonishing the British that "all men are created equal" while the Americans owned slaves. Jefferson included a paragraph on slavery in his rough drafts of the Declaration. According to Carl Becker, in his *The Declaration of Independence* (Alfred A. Knopf, Inc., 1922), it reads:

[The King of Great Britain] has waged cruel war against human nature itself, violating its most sacred rights of life and liberty in the persons of a distant people who never offended him, captivating and carrying them into slavery in another hemisphere, or to incur miserable death in their transportation thither. This practical warfare, the opprobrium of infidel powers, is the warfare of the Christian king of Great Britain, determined to keep open a market where men should be bought and sold, he has prostituted his negative for suppressing every legislative attempt to prohibit or to restrain this execrable commerce and that this assemblage of horrors might want no fact of distinguished die, he has not excited those very people to rise in arms among us and to purchase that liberty of which he has deprived them, by murdering the people upon whom he also obtruded them; thus paying off former crimes committed against the liberties of one people, with crimes which he urges them to commit against the lives of another.

At first glance, Jefferson's motives seem humanitarian. He wanted to end the "assemblage of horrors" and give slaves their deserved liberty. Yet a closer examination reveals that Jefferson feared that slaves might run to the British army. He thus had to make appeals to the slaves and attempt to show that the colonists were really their friends, even though most of the drafters of the Declaration of Independence themselves owned slaves.

The British, in fact, had begun a standard policy of inducing slaves to seek "freedom" and join the British army. It should not be forgotten that King George's army had troubles recruiting enough manpower from home—slaves were the alternative force. According to Fishel and Quarles's documentary history of *The Negro American:*

The policy of inviting slaves to repair to the Crown forces was initiated in November, 1775 by Lord Dunmore, last of the royal governors of Virginia. . . . The number of slaves who had tried to reach his lines was not lost on the British Command. Henceforth the solicitation of Negroes became standard policy.

Expediency—not moral conviction—was also the governing factor in Black acceptance into the Revolutionary army. At the beginning of the struggle, a pattern of exclusion had set in. Washington, commander of the Continental army, feared that acceptance into that army would encourage slaves to run from their oppressors. Harsh reality, though, made Washington and other Founding Fathers radically alter their orders. To quote again from *The Negro American:*

As it became increasingly difficult to raise volunteer forces, local and state recruiting officers were inclined to meet their quotas by sending Negroes to Washington's army. Quietly reversing its policy, the Continental command accepted all Negroes sent by the states. . . . A Black soldier was a common sight north of the Potomac after 1777.

Although Black Men helped the Revolutionaries by offering their lives on the battlefields of America, no consideration was given to their sacrifice when the Constitution was written. The authors of the Constitution, however, were

shrewd enough to realize that change was inevitable. Therefore, they included within the Constitution devices for its
revision and interpretation:

The judicial Power of the United States shall be vested in one
supreme Court, and in such inferior Courts as the Congress may
from time to time ordain and establish. . . .

The role of the judiciary, especially the Supreme Court, in
the use of the Constitution is the decisive one. It is the court
that interprets the Constitution—deciding in essence if it will
become stagnant or if it will be applied in a just and realistic
manner.

John Marshall, as Chief Justice of the Supreme Court, set
the original procedure in the case of *Marbury* v. *Madison* 1
Cranch 137 (1803) which firmly established the court's
right of judicial review. According to Benjamin Munn
Ziegler in the introduction to *Desegregation and the Supreme Court:*

The Supreme Court claimed this power as a matter of right—
something inherent in the very nature of the judicial process. The
Court might have referred to No. 78 of *The Federalist* wherein
Alexander Hamilton specifically claimed it to be the duty of the
Court "to declare all acts contrary to the manifest tenor of the
Constitution void" but for obvious reasons they preferred this
broader ground.

In the decision in *Marbury* v. *Madison,* Marshall wrote:

So if a law be in opposition to the constitution, if both the law
and the constitution apply to a particular case . . . the court must
determine which of these conflicting rules governs the case. This
is the very essence of judicial duty.

If then the courts are to regard the constitution, and the constitution is superior to any ordinary act of the legislature, the consti-

tution, and not such ordinary act, must govern the case to which they both apply.

Since that time, the Court has had the power to interpret the Constitution and to affect profoundly every aspect of American life. The Court has not always accepted this challenge and has often responded to political and economic pressures in its decisions. But the potential for justice still exists—it is up to the courts to determine if the potential will ever be realized.

After the doctrine of judicial review was established, a steady stream of cases reached the Supreme Court that questioned the constitutionality of federal acts, and none of these acts were decided to be unconstitutional. There was a period of sixty-one years, from 1796 to 1857, before the Supreme Court invalidated another act.

The case of *Dred Scott* v. *Sanford* 19 US 393 (1856) set a legal precedent that has survived—in spirit at least—to the present. Dred Scott, a Missouri slave, sued for his freedom after having lived with his master on the free territory of Louisiana and Illinois. After being returned to Missouri, he contended that, having lived on "free soil a period of time," he had become a free man. His claim was given added validity because the Missouri Compromise of 1820 had outlawed slavery in those territories.

The Scott case became a national morals test—a test of the fairness and equity of the American judiciary. It was, as well, a case that could determine whether slavery would be extended farther west.

Thus Dred Scott, a poor slave, provided the Supreme Court of the United States with its first real opportunity to fulfill its potential as the major force for positive social change in the nation. The Court failed. The Supreme Court,

THREE-FIFTHS OF A MAN

speaking through Justice Roger B. Taney, ruled that since Scott was a slave and by definition was not a citizen, he had no right to sue in a United States court. He had no right to the protection of the American Constitution. The Supreme Court in 1857 sentenced Dred Scott, as well as millions of other Black Americans, to years more of slavery and servitude—to years of subhuman status in the "land of the free and the home of the brave."

The Court ruled at the same time that the Missouri Compromise was unconstitutional—resulting in a situation in which a master could take his slave anywhere and still retain title, just as with any other piece of property. Their alleged reasoning was that it would be unconstitutional to outlaw the extension of slavery.

Chief Justice Taney went far beyond the issues directly involved in the Scott case to declare that even when a Black Man became free, he could not claim to be a citizen of the United States, and that Congress acted unconstitutionally by outlawing the extension of slavery to newly acquired or about to be acquired territories. Howard Meyer in *Colonel of the Black Regiment* (the life of Thomas Wentworth Higginson) quotes Higginson, a supporter of John Brown and staunch abolitionist, as saying that the federal administration, including the Supreme Court, for the most part, since 1789 had largely been in the hands of able men from the South. Ironically, it is likely that informed southerners expected to lose the case—even southerners knew that their case was legally indefensible. However, in order to maintain slavery, the Supreme Court struck down the Missouri Compromise. That was only the second time in fifty-four years that the Court had declared an act of Congress unconstitutional.

The Dred Scott decision offers a constitutional study in hypocrisy, weakness, and gutlessness. That decision con-

62

tributed greatly to the atmosphere that, when added to economic factors, made war between the North and South inevitable. The impact of that one decision—and the discredit it brought upon the Court—has not yet been overcome. Court historians confess that the Taney court was a proslavery court (a "hanging court," so to speak), vulnerable to political pressures and lacking in the quality of leadership necessary to meet the demands of the times.

The result of the Dred Scott decision was to give added impetus to the drive against slavery. The Dred Scott case had once again demonstrated the intolerability of a society in which human slavery exists. The case had provided even deeper inspiration to Black Men and to their few white allies like John Brown.

John Brown watched in agony as his nation flouted all standards of decency and morality, as western expansion continued over the corpses of red men and Black Men, as treaties were blatantly disregarded. Brown, who asserted that this country would never end slavery in response to moral suasion, was in Kansas forcefully freeing slaves and organizing for the liberation of others.

During May 8–10, 1858, a convention of Black Men, mostly former slaves, and a few whites met in Chatham, Canada, west. They intended, with the Reverend John Brown's guidance, to govern the areas they would liberate from slavery. The creation of a provisional constitution gave Brown's men a tangible goal—evidence that the ideal for which they would fight and probably die was indeed superior to the oppressive system they sought to replace.

Their constitution was in some respects more specific and to the point than the American Constitution, but it did not include any guarantees that were not in the original American Constitution and granted to American citizens in the first ten amendments. The superiority of Brown's constitu-

63

tion was in fact that Black Men would indeed be "equal under law."

The Preamble to that "Provisional Constitution and Ordinances for the People of the United States" is as follows:

Whereas slavery, throughout its entire existence in the United States, is none other than a most barbarous, unprovoked, and unjustifiable war of one portion of its citizens upon another portion—the only conditions of which are perpetual imprisonment and hopeless servitude or absolute extermination—in utter disregard and violation of those internal and self-evident truths set forth in our Declaration of Independence.

Therefore, we citizens of the United States, and the oppressed people who by a recent decision of the Supreme Court, are declared to have no rights which the white man is bound to respect, together with all other people degraded by the laws thereof, do, for the time being, ordain and establish for ourselves the following Provisional Constitution and Ordinances, the better to protect our persons, property, lives and liberties, and to govern our actions.

At Harpers Ferry the intensity of the drive for liberation increased the momentum of its beat. Then came the Civil War, for which the United States Supreme Court shares responsibility—for the callous decision in the Dred Scott case.

The Emancipation Proclamation issued by President Abraham Lincoln on January 1, 1863, freed only some of the slaves. Lincoln stated that such emancipation was a fit and necessary war measure—nothing more. It was intended to improve morale for the Union army, which had been severely defeated at Fredericksburg. Indeed it proved to be the single event that most influenced the outcome of the war. (This proclamation, of course, was later expanded and formalized as the Thirteenth and Fourteenth amendments to the Constitution.)

It is widely conceded that the war was won largely due to the action of Black Men freed by the Emancipation Proclamation to become soldiers in the Union army. Black Men provided the margin of victory for the North.

The Union had promised the Black Man freedom and equality—after victory. Blacks had fought mainly on the side of the Union. They had loyally fought on behalf of the national government, yet they received none of the respect, aid, or power accorded the traitors and former rebels—the white southerners.

In 1861, at the beginning of the Civil War, Black Men petitioned the Union to permit them to fight in that war. Not until white enlistments declined and the Union army lost battle after battle did the attitude of the northern generals change. James M. McPherson, in *The Negro's Civil War*, related how Black Men in Boston, Philadelphia, New York, and other cities attempted to enlist in the army without success. Necessity soon altered this policy. Some Black Men, such as Henry Cropper, said they "would never fight for the Union unless the government accepted Black Men on the same basis as whites." There were many Blacks who viewed the affair as a "white man's war," the outcome of which was of little consequence to them. Nevertheless, an estimated 180,000 Black Men joined the Union army only to be treated with rank discrimination—discrimination in pay, food, clothing, and rate or height of possible advancement.

Colonel T. W. Higginson, a white man who commanded a Black regiment, wrote to the New York *Tribune* on January 22, 1864 in an attempt to get equal pay and treatment for his men. Colonel Higginson's letter read, in part:

Sir. . . . No one can overstate the intense anxiety with which the officers of colored regiments in this Department are awaiting action from Congress in regard to arrears of pay of their men.

It is not a matter of dollars and cents only; it is a question of common honesty—whether the United States Government has sufficient integrity for the fulfillment of an explicit business contract. . . . Every one of them knows that he volunteered under an explicit written assurance from the War Department that he should have the pay of a white soldier. . . . I have not seen a proposition in Congress to pay colored soldiers, from date of enlistment, the same pay with white soldiers; and yet anything short of that is unequivocal breach of contract, so far as this regiment is concerned.

Meanwhile, the land sales are beginning, and there is danger of every foot of land being sold from beneath my soldiers' feet, because they have not the petty sum which the Government first promised and then refused to pay. . . .

There is nothing mean or mercenary about these men in general. Convince them that the Government actually needs their money, and they would serve it barefooted and on half rations, and without a dollar—for a time. But, unfortunately, they see white soldiers beside them, whom they know to be in no way their superiors for any military service, receiving hundreds of dollars for re-enlisting from this impoverished Government which can only pay seven dollars out of thirteen to its black regiments. And they see, on the other hand, those colored men who refused to volunteer as soldiers, and who have found more honest paymasters than the United States Goverment, now exulting in well-filled pockets, and able to buy the little homesteads the soldiers need, and to turn the soldiers' families into the streets. Is this a school for self-sacrificing patriotism?

Eventually Higginson petitioned Congress on behalf of his men. The War Department agreed to equal pay of thirteen dollars per month, which it paid for five months; it was then reduced to ten dollars, then to seven.

In the South, on the other hand, even Robert E. Lee recommended accepting Black Men into the army—provided that, with their masters consent, they were first made free. Such policy was adopted in March, 1865—too late materially to affect the result of the war.

Following the Civil War, the Black Men newly elected to the state legislatures were determined to achieve their freedom. The former slaves were uneducated and often inarticulate, but they knew what had been denied them as slaves and they knew what they wanted now that they were free. The primary goal of the freed slaves was public education. W. E. B. DuBois wrote in his classic work on this period, *Black Reconstruction:*

By straining his political power to the utmost, the Negro voter got a public school system and got it because that was one clear object which he understood and which no bribery or chicanery could seduce him from advocating and insisting upon in season and out. . . . He had . . . but one clear economic ideal and that was his demand for land, his demand that the great plantations be subdivided and given to him as his right. This was a perfectly fair and natural demand and ought to have been an integral part of Emancipation. To emancipate four million laborers whose labor had been owned, and separate them from the land upon which they had worked for nearly two and a half centuries, was an operation such as no modern country had for a moment attempted or contemplated. The German and English and French serf, the Italian and Russian serf, were, on emancipation, given definite rights in the land. Only the American Negro slave was emancipated without such rights and in the end this spelled for him the continuation of slavery.

The laws written by the former slaves during the brief years that they were in power were the most enlightened and progressive laws in America to date. DuBois wrote:

Indeed, the Negro voter in Reconstruction had disappointed all the prophets. . . . The Negro buttressed Southern civilization in precisely the places it was weakest, against popular ignorance, oligarchy in government, and land monopoly.

In spite of, or perhaps because of, this progressiveness, the white South remained unrepentant. Resistance to Black participation in the democratic processes hardened, and the southerners organized against the slaves. The whites demonstrated their solidarity by electing Confederate representatives to Congress in 1865. Among those elected, according to a tally by John Hope Franklin, were the vice-president of the Confederacy, four Confederate generals, five Confederate colonels, six Confederate cabinet officers, and fifty-eight members of the Confederate congress. Of course, these men were constitutionally barred from assuming office because they had participated in insurrection against the United States, but their elections vividly reaffirmed the stubborn attitude of the white southerners.

Although the Reconstruction Congress elected in 1865 managed to institute the Freedmen's Bureau over the veto of President Andrew Johnson, the amnesty proclamations of Lincoln and Johnson restored land to the former owners. Therefore, Black Americans were still landless and poor even after having fought in a war for their freedom and having suffered the barbarism of slavery.

The Ku Klux Klan was organized into the greatest force of terror in America to that time. Each year hundreds of Blacks were lynched or burned at the stake. The murderers were almost never punished. The Black Codes, instead of the

Constitution, had become the law of the land. These were laws whose roots rested firmly in the institution of slavery —which were designed to relegate Black Men to slavery permanently. The Black Codes had existed since 1619—that fateful year when the first boatload of slaves arrived in America. It was also the year of the first meeting of the House of Burgess in Virginia—this country's first meeting of the representative democracy. Slavery could not have been so effectively enforced without the support of laws like the Black Codes—laws that were written, implied, or adhered to by "gentlemen's agreement."

The Thirteenth and Fourteenth amendments should have automatically negated the effect of the Black Codes—the epitome of which was the decision in the Dred Scott case. Nevertheless, neither the courts nor the general American public would accept the obvious implications of those amendments. Public pressure and judicial irresponsibility, joined with the terrorism of the Klan, created an atmosphere that allowed the reinstitution of the Black Codes by 1865.

These codes were applied to restrict every area of the Black Man's life. Laws passed by many state legislatures restricting employment, housing, public accommodations, marriage, voting, suffrage, the bearing of arms, jury duty, and the possession of property were specifically applied to Black People. These written and unwritten laws enforced a social order in which white men need not compete with Black Men on any level.

Not until 1883 did cases reach the Supreme Court that tested the constitutionality of acts under the war amendments—the Thirteenth and Fourteenth amendments. Those amendments had been expressly written to grant to Black Men the same rights enjoyed by white people. A war in which many had suffered and died had been fought to establish these principles. Prior to their passage, these amendments had been thoroughly discussed in both houses of the Congress, by the national press, and by many contemporary writers. Members of both political parties knew and understood them. Again, on the state level, the amendments were debated. In fact, they had to be ratified by each of the Confederate states before the states could rejoin the Union. No one, including the former slaves, doubted the intent and purpose of those amendments. Apparently the only ones in doubt were the justices of the highest court in the land.

The first such cases reaching the Supreme Court were the Slaughterhouse cases 16 US 36 (1873). The state of Louisiana had granted a huge contract to a single butchering firm, and more than one thousand butchers objected in court. The granting of this monopoly was alleged to prevent smaller butchers from continuing in business. Relief was sought by reason of the Thirteenth and Fourteenth amendments to the United States Constitution.

Once again the Court vacillated—distinguishing between state citizenship and national citizenship, holding that the Thirteenth Amendment forbade physical slavery but not the oppression of monopolies. The Court held that federal citizenship did not include the protection of ordinary civil rights from infringement by state governments. The Court knew that this dangerous doctrine would leave the newly freed Blacks at the mercy of the former slavemasters who would determine and certainly restrict the civil rights of Black People. The Court knew that such economic monopolies would relegate Black People to an "involuntary condition of servitude." Nevertheless, it was the intent of the Court to reserve to the states the control of the civil rights of individuals.

The distinction between state citizenship and federal citizenship was allowed to permit white men to retain control of the politics and economy of the nation. This was done in spite of the fact that the Constitution clearly establishes the priority of the federal government over the state governments. This intention is made most explicit in Article 6:

This Constitution, and the Laws of the United States which shall be made in Pursuance thereof; and all Treaties made, or which shall be made, under the Authority of the United States, shall be the supreme Law of the Land; and the Judges in every State shall be bound thereby, any Thing in the Constitution or Laws of any State to the Contrary notwithstanding.

The Court's decision was presented in something of a tirade. It ruled that Congress could not create a municipal code and that the Fourteenth Amendment was limited in scope. The Court further reasoned that the Fourteenth Amendment was a prohibition against *state action:* "It is state action of a particular character that is prohibited. Individual rights are not the subject matter of the Amendment."

With that, the Court displayed its disregard for human beings in preference for the irrelevancies of abstract concepts, which invariably were used to benefit the monopolies. The Court also found that Congress does not have plenary power and that the refusal to serve Black People, a question of state rights, must be redressed in the state court. In the Civil Rights cases 109 US 3 (1883), it stated:

It would be running the slavery argument into the ground to make it apply to every act of discrimination which a person may see fit to make as to the guest he will entertain, or as to the people he will take into his coach or cab or car, or admit to his concert or theatre, or deal with in other matters of intercourse of business.

Would it? Or would it, instead, be utilizing the Constitution in its highest sense—using it to attack the most pervasive evils of the society? The systematic exclusion of a group or class of people from the economy cannot be tolerated in a "free" society. No amount of legalizing will make it tolerable.

71

The Civil Rights Acts of 1875 and 1876 were finally passed by virtue of the Fourteenth Amendment, Section 1. They stated:

That all persons within the jurisdiction of the United States shall be entitled to the full and equal enjoyment of the accommodations, advantages, facilities and privileges of inns, public conveyances on land or water, theatres, and other places of public amusement; subject only to the conditions and limitations established by law, and applicable alike to citizens of every race and color, regardless of any previous condition of servitude.

The Court declared the Civil Rights Acts of 1875 and 1876 unconstitutional and, in effect, null and void—extending the precedent set in the Slaughterhouse cases.

Mr. Justice Harlan delivered a brilliant dissent. He stated:

It is not the words of the law but the internal sense of it that makes the law; the letter of the law is the body; the sense and reason of the law is the soul. . . . The court has departed from the familiar rule requiring in the interpretation of constitutional provisions, that full effect be given to the intent with which they were adopted.

The Fourteenth Amendment represented one of the first instances in American history that Congress was empowered to enforce an express restriction upon the states. The Court had carefully used evasive language, not strong legal reasoning, to reach a decision that would further subject Black People to the oppression of the ruling class.

The decision of the Supreme Court in these early civil rights cases disturbed not only Black Men but all contemporary leaders of conscience. Frederick Douglass decried the decision at a public meeting in Washington. Douglass equated the decision with the news "that the National Capitol had been surrendered to Jefferson Davis." In his autobiography Douglass said:

The future historian will turn to the year 1883 to find the most flagrant example of this national deterioration. . . . Whatever this Supreme Court may have been in the past, or may by the Constitution have been intended to be, it has, since the days of the Dred Scott decision, been wholly under the influence of the slave power.

Douglass gave a brilliant analysis at that meeting of the views of concerned leadership—Black and white. He represented effectively most of the other Black Leaders of the time.

There is a great deal of historical data available to suggest a conspiracy to strip Black Men of power. According to DuBois: "The Democrats promised to guarantee 'peace, good order, protection of the law to whites and blacks'; or, in other words, exploitation should be so quiet, orderly and legal, as to assure regular profit to Southern owners and Northern investors."

Arthur Kinoy, in "The Constitutional Right," *Rutgers Law Review*, states:

The Bradley Court, reflecting the profound changes which had occurred in the nation in the immediate years following the fateful decisions of 1877 [the Civil Rights cases that interpreted the Civil Rights Acts], faced the immensely difficult task of constructing a legal rationale which could justify the conclusion already reached by the new national political majority—that the primary responsibility for the enforcement of the rights of freedmen was to be turned over to the individual southern states. The Compromise of 1877 represented a decision to abandon in the political arena the concept of national responsibility for the enforcement of the newly created rights of the race of freedmen.

After the landmark Civil Rights cases of 1883, the Court ruled in the Ku Klux Klan cases (*ex parte* Yarbrough) 110 US 651 (1884). Yarbrough and other Klan members were convicted of conspiring to intimidate Berry Saunders, a Black

73

Man, and preventing him from exercising his constitutional right to vote in a federal election. The men were convicted under the Enforcement Act of 1870, which forbade the conspiracy to injure or threaten any citizen in the free exercise of rights secured to him by the Constitution.

This interpretation was still extremely limited and inadequate in that it applied only to federal elections. The Supreme Court upheld Yarbrough's conviction. The Court held the federal statute valid—that the right to vote for congressional representatives was a federal right under the dual citizenship theory, not a state right, and was protected under the Constitution.

This ruling did not, unfortunately, repudiate the former rulings establishing differences between state and national citizenship. The only valid decision would have been one that recognized only one form of citizenship, i.e., citizenship in the United States of America, and recognized that the country a man is forced to fight and die for, that the country to which he must pledge allegiance, owes him the rights of human dignity.

The federal government has only rarely and reluctantly used the powers granted to it in Article 6 of the Constitution, which grants supremacy to the federal government over state governments. On a few occasions federal troops have been called to enforce the edicts requiring integration of southern schools and colleges, as in the case of the University of Mississippi. But in most instances the government has adopted a *laissez-faire* attitude toward the states and has left them to do as they wished with Black People.

Following Reconstruction, once again the Supreme Court acted to reinforce and perpetuate racism while ignoring opportunities to imbue in the nation a moral commitment and dedication to justice. The court system has repeatedly been used to advance the racism of America and to prevent Blacks from obtaining the power that is rightfully theirs. The classic example of this is the decision of *Plessey* v. *Ferguson* 163 US 537 (1896). The Court held that a Louisiana statute requiring railroads to "provide equal but separate accommodations for the white and colored races," did not constitute a denial of the Fourteenth Amendment, which granted "equal protection of the laws" to all citizens.

The law was ruled a proper exercise of a state's police powers aimed at the maintenance of peace and order. The Court dismissed the contention that the "enforced separation of the two races stamps the colored race with the badge of inferiority" and observed, "if this be so, it is not by reason of anything foul in the act, but solely because the colored race chooses to put that construction upon it."

This decision was particularly insidious in view of the racist social structure of America. For in a racist society in which one race is in control, "separate but equal" can never be a reality. It is apparent that the decision of *Plessey* v. *Ferguson* was intended to provide time. The decision no doubt did further psychological damage to an already sick nation by giving a false legitimacy to segregation—a segregation which could not possibly provide for equality.

During the Reconstruction period everyone was certainly aware that the Black Man was not really free—he had no land, no property, no rights. He was less than an alien in this country.

Therefore, when the Supreme Court made its historic ruling, the judges did so knowing that Black Men in America would receive none of the protections of the system. They must have known that the Black Codes would be declared illegal before the turn of the century; therefore, the decision could serve to reinforce the racist system. The Black Man did not have a chance.

The doctrine of separate but equal was extended in the case of *Berea College* v. *Kentucky* 211 US 45 (1908). The Court held that the state could forbid a college, even though a private corporation, to teach whites and Blacks at the same time and place, leaving no doubt about the validity of the southern state laws regarding education of white children and Black children in separate tax-supported schools. The *Plessey* v. *Ferguson* doctrine was extended to every aspect of southern life, denying the Black Man the basic rights of citizenship.

Several years later, after some of the judges sitting at the time of the *Plessey* v. *Ferguson* case had died and been replaced, the Supreme Court did begin to require some evidence that separate was indeed equal. The court was extremely lenient, however, in its definition of "equal." It held that the term meant not exact mathematical equality but substantial equality.

Thus, in the case of *Cummings* v. *the Board of Education* 175 US 528 (1899), the Court found no denial of equal protection under the laws in the failure of a southern county to provide a high-school education for sixty Black children—although it provided a high school for the white children. The Court seemed to be satisfied with the county's explanation that it couldn't afford a high school for Black children.

It was not until 1914, in the case of *McCabe* v. *the Atchison, Topeka and Santa Fe Railway Company* 235 US 151 (1914), that an Oklahoma law was held invalid because it allowed the railroads to haul sleeping, dining, and chair cars exclusively for the use of white people without providing them for Black People upon their demand.

From 1896 to 1954 the standard of "separate" was unfailingly applied but the standard of "equal" only rarely.

Therefore, the doctrine of "separate but equal" was never given a chance, for "equal" would have implied control by indigenous people. And the social order of the United States would have been "separation"—not "segregation."

The Court, in the case of *Ex rel. Gaines* v. *Canada* 305 US 337 (1938), finally made a dramatic move forward when it decided that Gaines, a Black Man who had sought admission to the state law school in Missouri, could not be denied admission. Chief Justice Hughes held that the student was, in the absence of other provisions, entitled to be admitted to the law school of the state university, even though the state had offered to pay his tuition at some out-of-state law school.

It is constitutionally stated, as the Supreme Court correctly noted, that Congress has certain powers, among these to regulate interstate commerce. All Congress had done was to forbid any interstate carrier to give any person or group any "unreasonable preference or advantage" or subject them to any prejudice or disadvantage. Nevertheless, the Southern Railway Company continued to segregate Black passengers. Most of the tables in the dining cars were reserved for whites. Only two tables were allowed for Blacks, and these were cordoned off by a curtain.

In *Henderson* v. *the U.S.* 339 US 816 (1950) the Court held such segregation subjugated Black passengers to undue prejudice and disadvantage and was an "unreasonable preference or advantage" to white people. It was not until 1950 that the Court reached this decision—a bit late.

If "separation" had actually been tried, the thrust for integration might never have been necessary—or it may have already become, at least educationally and politically, a reality. For the southern states would have found that maintenance of two equal systems was prohibitively expensive and would, of necessity, have been forced to revert to integration. For it is not integration that is necessary. It is the protection of equal rights, equal protection under laws, and the right to freedom of choice.

In 1954 the case of *Brown* v. *the Board of Education*, combined with the case of *Bowdoin* v. *Sharp* 347 US 483 (1954), upset the doctrine of "separate but equal." The Supreme Court took fifty-eight years from the first mistaken decision to decide that the doctrine of "separate but equal" was invalid and unworkable. It took the Supreme Court fifty-eight years to understand what "separate" meant; it took that long for it to discover what "equal" meant. It took the Supreme Court fifty-eight years to recognize its responsibility to America.

The Court, in *Brown* v. *the Board of Education*, ruled:

In the cases dealing with Negro segregation that reached the Supreme Court after Plessey vs. Ferguson, the doctrine of that case was followed but never re-examined. The Court seemed content with the "separate but equal" rule of the case which, as someone aptly put it, guarantees to the Negro "the equal but different," protection of the laws.

This decision ended a forty-year period beginning in 1914 with the McCabe case, during which time the Court applied ever more rigid standards of equality under segregation— finding that the Black plaintiffs had, in each case, been denied equality of treatment. An attempt at judicial realism had finally been made.

The Court, adhering to a "rule of construction" or judicial self-restraint that avoids the decision of constitutional issues whenever possible, continued to spoon-feed relief to the Blacks, in small doses, without ever challenging the basic evils of the system. The Court has the option to change this rule if it so desires. The abandonment of the rule would deeply and affirmatively affect the basic protection of the constitutional rights of Black People.

An infinitely better guide would be to decide all constitutional issues first—with all other issues receiving secondary priority. Surely, unless the constitutional question is given preference over lesser questions, it can never be "the Supreme Law of the Land." This rule could be applied wherever a constitutional question is raised—particularly under the Thirteenth and Fourteenth amendments. The Court should be committed to examine the case to determine if there is probable cause that the complaint violates the Thirteenth Amendment, the Fourteenth Amendment, or the Bill of Rights.

If the Supreme Court would advance all cases alleging violation of constitutional rights to the dockets first, this would cut down the amount of time and money involved in the disposition of cases.

With the decision in the case of Brown v. *the Board of Education,* the Court took a giant step toward realizing its potential. It ruled on constitutional issues but it took into account the way in which the issues would be applied in daily American life. It was a proud moment in the history of American jurisprudence, but it only lasted a little while.

Since that decision, the Court has only occasionally displayed the brilliance of which it is capable.

In June of 1968, the Supreme Court rendered an opinion in a housing bias case, *Jones* v. *Mayer Co.,* that legally ended all justification for discrimination in the sale or rental of property, on racial or religious grounds. Justice Potter Stewart stated in the majority opinion:

In this case we are called upon to determine the scope and the constitutionality of an Act of Congress, 42 USC, Section 1982, which provides that:

"All citizens of the United States shall have the same rights, in every state and territory, as are enjoyed by white citizens thereof,

79

to inherit, purchase, lease, sell, hold or convey real and personal property . . ."

At the very least, the freedom that Congress is empowered to secure under the Thirteenth Amendment includes the freedom to buy whatever a white man can buy, the right to live wherever a white man can live. If Congress cannot say that being a free man means at least this much, then the Thirteenth Amendment made a promise the nation cannot keep.

That decision, applying a law passed during the Reconstruction period, more than any other recent decision, demonstrated that the power for liberation exists. The laws are already on the books, albeit unenforced. The rhetoric and fanfare accompanying the Civil Rights Bill of 1968, which provided only watered-down fair-housing clauses, was false and unnecessary. Well-intentioned activists would do better to direct their efforts to seeing that existing laws—such as those passed by Reconstruction Congresses—are enforced.

The abundance of civil-rights bills passed in the 1960's were all unnecessary. The authority granted to the government by those bills already exists in the Constitution. These civil-rights bills did more for Congressional public relations than for Blacks. If the Presidents and the courts during this time had truly wanted to enforce the Constitution and the Declaration of Independence, they could have done so without turning to Congress.

If these superfluous bills had been enforced, it would have justified their passage. But they, too, have been allowed to drown in a sea of indifference. The mere passage of laws solves *nothing*—only their implementation would address the problem. The Fourteenth Amendment provides:

Neither slavery nor involuntary servitude, except as a punishment for crime whereof the party shall have been duly convicted shall exist within the United States, or any place subject to this jurisdiction.

Most Black People still live in "an involuntary condition of servitude." They are the victims of a system of economic, political, and social slavery. If America is to give life to the Constitution, slavery of every form must be abolished. This cannot be done unless Black People are given a stake in the economy, as well as the political system. It necessitates the transfer of ghetto property to the Black Community. If men are not able to control the economies of their communities, they will necessarily remain in "an involuntary condition of servitude" to their landlords and their bosses. They will be unable to break the cycle of oppression and make the Constitution viable.

The American legal system badly abuses all poor people, and in America most Blacks are poor and many of the poor are Black. The poor are, by virtue of their economic condition, relegated to a form of involuntary servitude. They do not have an equal option on "life, liberty and the pursuit of happiness."

If the Court honestly intends to help make a new society, the "equal protection of the laws" must be extended to cover the most ordinary and, to white people, unimportant instances of discrimination. If Black Men are ever to have a stake in America, they must be treated, in every respect, as well as whites. In a racist society, this means that there may have to be compensatory efforts made by the government —federal and state agencies—to see that equality of service is protected.

For example, in urban America, Black People are daily denied taxi service by fearful, racist, white cab drivers who will not service ghetto areas. They are daily inconvenienced, insulted, and maligned by hack drivers who will not do their jobs. There is no immediate, effective court of appeals. Taxi cabs provide a public service. Authority to operate a cab is issued by the city, and, theoretically, standards of operation are set by the city. They are supposed to be set and enforced in such a way as to guarantee service to all citizens and in such a way as to preclude discrimination of any sort.

Penalties for discrimination by cab drivers must be severe. The failure to serve Black People simply because they are Black is *not* a misdemeanor, but a criminal act, and must be dealt with as such. Strong fines—even still, jail sentences —must be meted out to public servants who will not serve the Black public.

Public taxis have no more right than Transit Authority buses or Greyhound buses to choose passengers. They have no authority to choose the destinations of their passengers. Therefore, when hacks refuse to drive a Black person, whether to a ghetto area or elsewhere, the city agencies must move swiftly.

It will probably be necessary, in most cities, in order to free the taxi industry from racism, to restructure the entire industry and to redistribute power for controlling the industry. A hack authority located in the Black Community, run by Black Men from that community and with the ability to penalize cab drivers from its own jurisdiction as well as other jurisdictions, would be an answer.

The privileges and immunities clause of the Fourteenth Amendment guarantees every citizen the same protection and privileges as any other citizen. In a situation in which an entire segment of the population is systematically denied its rights over and over again, the state must take positive steps to remedy the situation. Mere provision of a complaint bureau or a state human-relations commission isn't enough; the situation must be stopped, and it is the responsibility of the state to stop it.

Many whites scoff at the suggestion that taxi service could involve a constitutional issue. I contend, however, that every time a Black Man is refused service, assistance, or advice simply on the basis of his Blackness, a constitutional right is violated. It is this kind of daily hurt and insult that creates the kind of hopelessness and despair that erupts in ghetto rebellions.

The death penalty—that most cruel and inhumane punishment—must be abolished. It has historically been used in a discriminatory manner. The Supreme Court has so far upheld the right of the states to kill men convicted of certain crimes. Statistically, more Blacks than whites are executed for these crimes. This is a hangover from slavery and the residue of the Black Codes and the era of unrestricted lynchings.

There are certain crimes punishable by death in most southern states. The crimes are rape, murder, arson, and burglary in the night. In states where slavery did not exist, the death penalty has either been abolished or is reserved for only one or two offenses, such as murder and rape.

Statistics from two states, North Carolina and Maryland, demonstrate how the death penalty has been employed in a discriminatory manner. In North Carolina, for example, between the years of 1909 and 1934, 153 whites were executed for murder as compared to 392 Black Men. Fourteen whites were executed for rape while 110 Black Men were executed; for the crime of burglary, 3 white men were executed, 38 Black men were killed. And in North Carolina, less than 40 percent of the population is Black.

In Maryland during a period from 1940 to 1966 the state executed forty-seven persons for capital offences. Of those executed, seven were white and the other forty were Black Men. Joseph C. Howard, Sr., writes in his *Administration of*

*Rape Cases in the City of Baltimore and the State of Maryland* (Monumental Bar Association, 1967):

Examination of the figures of Table II reveals that of the fifty-five recipients of the death penalty since 1923, all but two either directly or indirectly involved white females. It is further quite obvious that in Maryland no man white or black, has ever been executed for the rape of a Negro female.

These facts, to all but the most biased, would indicate the extent to which Blacks—men and women—are denied the "equal protection of the laws."

Southern states rewrote their constitutions and criminal laws to control Black People. Most of the laws made during this period were racist and unconstitutional and remain so today. The rules of evidence were ignored in trials. If a white woman in the South charges rape, there is little likelihood that the Black Man involved will be cleared. Many Black Men on the chain gangs have been unjustly sentenced. The action of the courts and the judiciary (who refuse to admit Black lawyers in the South, for example, into their professional organizations) have not yet convinced Black People that they will actually enforce the law. If a Black Man, the victim, knows he cannot get justice and the white man knows he can get "judgment" by virtue of his white power, white lawlessness is encouraged. Neither the Blacks nor the whites can have respect for the court.

A thorough knowledge of the law is valuable to any man forced to deal with a society as complex as modern America. For the Black Man, it is essential. Black Men are daily faced with violations of their rights; they are faced with discrimination and illegality. Without a knowledge of their rights, they cannot possibly defend themselves against exploitation;

without a knowledge of their rights, they cannot possibly live as men.

Even poor whites do not have to rely on the law for protection as do Black People. Their skin color affords them a measure of protection and acceptance Black People lack. Even exploitation of white by white is not as great as Black by white.

The entire legal hierarchy in America—including federal, state, and municipal judges, elected and appointed, as well as the lawyers and law-enforcement officials—all share in the responsibility for bringing about social change in this country. The lesser courts as well as the Supreme Court are charged with equal responsibility. The executive no less than the judicial branch must see to it that court decisions are enacted and legal provisions enforced. We must keep in mind Andrew Jackson's famous retort to the Supreme Court when it commanded him to act. "Justice Marshall has made his decision" he said, "now let him enforce it."

With the cities burning, with America's house burning down, with racism festering in every pocket of American life, men in all branches of the government must become "social engineers."

Those who control the administration of the law control the destiny—individually and collectively—of the entire population. Their control over the Black Community is more absolute than over any other group because that community has the fewest legal resources for its own defense.

In a society in which money is the supreme value, the legal system is irrelevant to the rich, except the use of court decisions in profit-making ventures. By virtue of their expensive lawyers, hearings are guaranteed to the rich for every grievance, and if their wealth is sufficient, they will be above the law. As Cornelius Vanderbilt noted, "What do I care about the law? Hain't I got the power?"

However, in our society the legal system is very relevant to the poor and to the colored. It is the legal system that exercises the authority of freedom and bondage, life and death. The judiciary—and particularly the Constitution—is very important to Black Men. It is their only hope for social justice without chaos.

Among Black People the American legal apparatus is regarded with distrust and fear. Too often Black people have received unfair and biased judgments. Too often white juries have awarded Black Men less compensation than white men for similar complaints and injuries. Too often Black Men have been manhandled, mistreated, and insulted by officers of the law and officers of the courts. Too often cases brought to court by Black plaintiffs have been summarily dismissed for "insufficient evidence" while similar cases brought by white men have been tried and frequently decided in favor of the plaintiff.

I have personally been aware of many instances of cruelty by white police officers toward defendants who are poor and Black. It is not uncommon for Black "suspects" to be relieved of their money by the police and then made to sign waivers stating that their property has been returned. Often the "suspect" cannot even read what he is ordered to sign. If the case ever reaches court, signed statements are accepted as an unimpeachable defense.

Black Men do not have to cite statistics. They do not have to approach the matter scientifically. They know. They have been mistreated. They have seen their families and friends mistreated. Such experience can breed only disrespect, even hatred, for the law.

There are extremely few Black court officers or lawyers and even fewer Black judges. This is significant because judges are among the most powerful men in this society, often exercising the right of life or death, at least in the case of the poor and the Black. When the man wielding that power is racist, the most appalling miscarriages of justice occur—in both North and South.

Judges are usually instruments of the status quo rather than social engineers able to combat oppression. They are invariably tied to middle- or upper-class values. And for the poor man in society, whether he is white or Black, the most powerful officials are not those within the prestigious, white marble walls of the Supreme Court or even in the state courts, but rather the first judge in the municipal system —the county judge or the judge in the magistrate's court. Poor people usually are unable to make appeals; costs are prohibitive.

The American system of law is based on the English tradition. In England, law is the profession of the rich. How much justice one gets generally depends upon how much money one has. Thus, in many instances, even when a traffic ticket is given to a person, whether the ticket is justified or not, it is too expensive in time and cost to secure equality before the law. There are thousands of cases in which poor people lose three days work and more just to find out on what date their case will be tried.

The influence of politics on the courts is disastrous. It is common for political parties to control the nomination and appointment of judicial candidates. This is a dangerous, undemocratic practice; too often judgeships are passed out to political hacks who by chance hold law degrees. The payment of favors must not be sufficient qualification for the bench. This common practice, moreover, has kept the judiciary white, for few party bosses would appreciate being known as the man who arranged an appointment for a Black judge. Consequently the judiciary has fewer Black Men than any other position, with the exception of Presidency of the

United States. Of course, Black people *do* serve menial jobs in the courts as they do everywhere in this country. But there are few Black judges in the United States and very few poor judges—financially speaking.

The type of judges resulting from political appointments are exemplified by some of the choices made by President John F. Kennedy, generally conceded to be a "liberal." They include J. Robert Talmadge in Georgia ("I don't want these pinks, radicals and black voters to outvote those who are trying to preserve our segregationist laws and other traditions"); William Cox in Mississippi ("I'm not interested in whether the registrar is going to give a registration test to a bunch of niggers on a voter drive"); Clarence W. Allgood in Alabama, who expelled from school 1,100 Black children for participating in civil-rights demonstrations; E. Gordon West in Louisiana ("I personally regard the 1954 holding of the United States Supreme Court in the now famous Brown case as one of the truly regrettable decisions of all times"); and Frank Ellis in Louisiana, who revived the old trick of indicating a candidate's race on the ballot. In Howard Zinn's *SNCC: The New Abolitionists*, from which these examples were taken, it is reported that Robert Kennedy, then Attorney General, said of these appointments of segregationists: "I'm very proud of the judges that have been appointed. We looked into all of them for questions of integrity and whether they would uphold the law of the land."

The American judicial system is largely a system of precedents. The criteria most frequently applied to court decisions is "Has it been done before?" Such a measure is hardly a progressive guide. It is the courageous judge who applies the better yardstick: "Is it just?" "Will it work?" and "Does it further the real intentions of the Constitution?"

The law is only as good and valid as are those who must

uphold it—the judges; and it is only as good and valid as the people believe it to be. Lawyers and judges with values no better than the white masses—an *ipso facto* commitment to racism and material values, lacking a strong commitment to the individuals they must protect and to the Constitution as the supreme law of the land—are unable to help insure honest equal protection before the law. Respect for the purpose of law lies within the minds of lawyers and others who enforce it; without the commitment of these people, all citizens stand in peril. And the Black man today stands in mortal danger.

Largely as a result of reactionary schooling and middle-class backgrounds, American judges and lawyers are among the most conservative members of their society. And they are almost without exception racist, often unconsciously. This conservatism makes it difficult for laws to be anything more than a reactionary device for preserving the status quo, regardless of the not-too-frequent progressive decisions made by the Supreme Court. It also creates a situation in which it is difficult for Black militants to secure dedicated lawyers who will imaginatively defend them. The few such lawyers who are both willing and able are already severely overtaxed.

Our legal system is part of the capitalistic system and has acted as an unswerving support for that system. An individual who grows up under its influence almost invariably has a capitalistic—and racist—orientation. It is difficult to produce the kind of people who will move for change or who believe that capitalism, because it feeds racism, is in need of change. After four years of undergraduate work and three years of law school, most come out believing that the American legal system is workable and just. Many Americans, even "educated" Americans, do not believe that the system exploits, and believe that the reason Blacks have not progressed is because they lack "basic skills" and aptitudes. The most basic skill—the most rewarding aptitude—is being born white.

Most judges and lawyers are products of white middle-class and upper-class America. They have been protected from any contact with the harsh reality of America's Black ghettos. They have been taught—and they have learned well —popular stereotypes and prejudices.

If America is to save itself, it must do so through a legal system that is designed to aid Black Men and poor men and represent their interests. In order to create such a system, a new type of lawyer is necessary—a social engineer, an agent for progress. We cannot wait for America to psychoanalyze itself. Unbiased legalism is the way to mediate between men. We need dedicated social engineers to point the way.

If Black People are ever to gain respect for the American judiciary, they must know that it is administered, at least in part, by Black Men. They must know that representatives of the Black Community are heard in the courts of the land —and that they have power and influence. The courts in which Black People are most frequently tried—local magistrates' courts—should be in the Black Community. When laws are invariably enforced "downtown," Black People cannot feel that the legal system is responsive to them. Courthouses must stand in Harlem and Bedford Stuyvesant as well as among the towers of Wall Street.

More important, the Black lawyers and judges must be of high caliber. They must be imbued with a regard and concern for people. They must not be "creamed" by white law schools—chosen not for their commitment to their people but for their dedication to white values. There are a few such men already available and working for justice.

In order to produce quantities of Black Men to serve in

the judiciary, the methods for training and education must be drastically revamped. The current method for educating lawyers severely restricts the chances of any man joining the bar who is not white as well as middle class. The demand of seven years' schooling precludes most poor people—Black and white—from entering the legal establishment. It is not realistic to demand that poor people suspend most of their earning capacity to study for a goal seven years away.

Many middle-class youngsters are preconditioned to expect years of professional training. Their parents are usually able to finance completely or at least in part their children's education. Middle-class parents are oriented to expect to support their children even past the age of twenty-one. In poor families it is often necessary for children to fend for themselves, sometimes even helping to support their younger brothers and sisters.

Minimally, there must be programs established in which poor people can study and work at the same time. It is not enough to educate those who already possess language skills and adequate educational backgrounds to study law. Remedial programs must be included, and Black People who have been educationally crippled by an oppressive system must be rehabilitated. We cannot wait for an entirely new generation to grow up before initiating change.

An important psychological factor negatively affecting poor children is that there is rarely someone from their own community who can serve as an example for the poor child. The lack of such a figure is even more acute for the Black child. The combined economic, political, and social forces have prevented other poor Blacks from "success" in a white world. Black youngsters now growing up are given little incentive to think that they can break the pattern. Other groups of immigrants—the Jews, the Germans, the Irish, the Poles—imported a few ready-made "successes" to serve as heroes for their children. Europeans brought high hopes; they came of their own volition and they came as families. Youngsters growing up on the Lower East Side thirty years ago generally regarded poverty as a temporary condition—a situation that could be remedied by hard work and education. But young Blacks living in the South and in the urban ghettos have seen their parents and other Blacks work hard for years. And they have seen them grow old and stagnate —still poor.

There will undoubtedly be great resistance within the establishment to the prospect of comparatively large numbers of poor Blacks entering the professions. In a nation of status seekers, the mere idea that a white middle-class profession might be "invaded" by the lower classes is enough to repel professionals from any attempts at social change.

The judges and juries who today interpret and apply the Constitution have had no special training to understand their own racism or the racism of others. White judges go to the same schools and read the same textbooks as the most vehement and outspoken racists.

As now constituted, the legal fraternity is inbred and self-perpetuating. Among the most prosperous and respected law firms are family concerns—partnerships of father and son, brothers and cousins. Many southern bar associations have just recently opened to admit Black People, and in the entire South there are, in 1968, less than five judges who are Black.

In order to alleviate the stagnation caused by this inbreeding, it will be necessary to infuse the professions with new people from the most disadvantaged communities. It will be necessary to avoid the classic pitfall of infusing these new professionals with the values of the middle class, causing them to reject their origins. The most valuable commodity in any disadvantaged community is the indigenous professional

—that man who can serve as a role model for children of the community as well as providing the adults with trusted assistance and leadership.

In order to make existing law schools effective—whether those law schools serve predominantly Black, predominantly white, or integrated student bodies—drastic changes will have to be made immediately. Faculties must be expanded to include urban planners, sociologists, and psychologists, as well as others expert in diversified fields. Students must be made to realize their responsibility for social change. Such realization will not be impressed upon them by stodgy professors steeped in the traditions of the precedent-ridden legal establishment.

Students of constitutional law must be made especially aware of the potential of the Constitution; they must be made aware of the power and force that could be exerted by this document. And they must be encouraged to interpret that document in ways pertinent to today's world.

In recent years there have been attempts to close even the few remaining Black law schools. It is said that Black law schools are costly, a burden on the taxpayer, and that their graduates are not as well educated or as prepared to practice law as their white counterparts. It is true that a lower percentage of graduates from Black schools pass bar examinations on the first try (hardly surprising in view of inadequate education provided for Blacks on every level—elementary, high school, college, and professional—and in view of the inferior facilities provided for Black students).

The fact that these Black schools are inadequate is no excuse to abandon them. They are one of the few remaining hopes to help salvage America, and they provide an excellent nucleus from which to develop necessary programs. These schools can be expanded and improved.

There are less than ten Black law schools in the nation.

Legislators—especially southern legislators—actively discourage establishment of new Black law schools or expansion of those in existence. They fear an influx of new Black lawyers into the courts. They are afraid that the effect of young Black Men trained in legal skills and committed to their people will limit the power of the establishment and have an ultimately liberalizing effect upon the court system. This fear has prompted many southern legislators to attempt to close the few Black law schools that exist—those few opportunities for advancement available to Black Men in America.

These white southerners have sometimes been aided unwittingly by northern liberals whose rationale for obstructing these young people from an education is ostensibly humanitarian. It is reasoned that if integration is the goal, segregated Black law schools are undesirable. This view was reinforced by the Supreme Court in the case of *Sweat* v. *Plainer* 339 US 629 (1950).

In that case the state of Texas claimed that its new law school for Black People offered educational opportunities essentially equal to those at the University of Texas Law School. The plaintiff, Sweat, had made an application to the University of Texas Law School. The court denied the claim of "equality at the Negro school" on the grounds that the law school for white students "possessed to a far greater extent those qualities which are incapable of objective measure but which make for greatness in a law school. The law school, the proving ground for legal learning and practice, cannot be effective in isolation from the individuals and institutions with which the law interacts."

The court ruled on the basis of the evidence at hand. In view of that evidence, the decision was a wise one. Nevertheless, there is no reason to believe that Black schools must always be inferior any more than Catholic or Jewish schools

94

must be inherently inferior. Black schools have historically been bad not because they are Black but because they have been inadequately financed and because the students have had no other alternative. They have had to make do with inferior education because it was the only kind available to them. It is likely, however, that with money and ingenuity these schools can be made to be among the best in the nation.

The role of the Supreme Court is a special one: it is the ultimate interpreter of the Constitution. Members of the Court must be of Olympian stature and should represent the highest quality of leadership that this country can produce —educated, intelligent, and egalitarian. They must be men committed to the protection of the Constitution, for, in reality, the Constitution and the Supreme Court are one and the same—and when the structure of one is under attack, so is the other. This is not to imply that the Court should ever be above criticism. The value of a free society is that none of its institutions can be above criticism or question. As James Baldwin has said: "I love America more than any other country in the world, and, exactly for this reason, I insist on the right to criticize her perpetually."

The Court must be stacked for justice and it must exercise all of the rights and powers granted to it under the Constitution. Yet it is painfully obvious to those of us who are still regarded as three-fifths of a man that the Constitution and the Supreme Court have not assumed their rightful roles. The Constitution is now under the guardianship of traditional liberals and conservatives—principally white men with views that conform to popular white American thought. Their appreciation of law, of course, is more profound and their understanding of legal precedents and maneuvers more exacting. But they have not seen fit to apply the Constitution in a revolutionary way.

In spite of the great power of the Court, it has been shown that the Supreme Court cannot force change without the cooperation and accord of the entire federal, state, and local judicial, executive, and legislative systems. But even alone, by good decisions and opinions and enforcement, the Court can force America to confront itself and can lead the way to progress and decency under law.

# PART 3
## Program and Peoplehood

## *Nobody In the World Is Better Than Us*

Now listen to what I'm outlining to you
Negroes who fought in World War I and II,
Some lose their life or they lose their hand
Still is fighting for the United Nations.

If Negroes were good enough to fight
Why can't we get a little equal rights.
For God made us all and in him we trust
Nobody in this world is better than us.

Why don't you folks realize without one another
As the Scriptures says "Love thy Neighbor."
If you be Jewish or Italian,
Negroes subject to Great Britain.

One thing folks should all realize
Six feet of dirt makes us all one size.
For God made us all and in him we trust
Nobody on earth is better than us.

I've been hearing you speak about this old Diplomacy
And Old Hypocrisy says I think
It's about time, you should cut it out
The way Negroes is treated down south.

In My opinion it's a rotten shame
Like they want to bring back slavery again.
For God made us all and in him we trust
For nobody in this world is better than us,
Nobody in this world is better than us.

—Hudie Leadbelly

THERE ARE TWO essential instruments that, if used to-
gether, if used to compliment each other, could save
America from destruction. They are the Constitution of the
United States, which necessarily includes the Declaration of
Independence, and the doctrine of Black Nationalism.

The philosophy of Black Nationalism has been developed
by a people with a history of oppression and suffering—a
history dominated by the twin brothers of inequity and
degradation. It is a philosophy that is in harmony with the
principles of the Constitution and that, if translated into action, can make those principles real for Black as well as
white America.

There has been a great deal of misunderstanding about
the nature and development of Black Nationalism in America. In flagrant disregard of the truth, the mass media have
misrepresented the teachings of Black Nationalists to mean
"Black racism" or "Black extremism." The meaning of
Black Nationalism has been distorted by white America and
certain of its Negro lackeys to mean segregation and race
hatred—even though its true goals are unity and pride, self-
respect and integrity.

White fear of Black Nationalism is illogical when viewed
in historical context, for historically nationalism means
simply a commitment to a group, a sense of responsibility to
one's own kind. Sometimes it is demonstrated by loyalty to a
country or state, sometimes by devotion to the traditions of
one's forefathers. Black Nationalism in America continues
in a tradition centuries old, adapting historical forms to the
needs and desires of today.

Nationalism is a prerequisite for statehood, and member-
ship in a state is imperative if a man is to have self-respect, if
he is to command the respect of other men.

Americans reserve profound sympathy for the "man without a country." American literature is rich with nationalistic lore. Yet the sympathy extended the "man without a country" is hardly ever extended to the millions of men who have no country today—America's displaced Black Men.

Most whites as well as Blacks know that the term "Negro American" is really no more than a means of identification for those Black People living in America, descended from slaves. Their status is not that of Americans. They are not treated as free men, nor are they recognized as such.

Throughout history men have felt a need for group identity—a need to relate directly to people like themselves, with common interests and bonds. Even from earliest recorded time, men roamed the earth in tribes—rarely alone. These tribes were formed partly for protection, partly for companionship.

In time most men settled down to raise their families and crops on designated pieces of land. Usually whole tribes adopted a land area—the people living and working together for mutual benefit and protection. These tribes sometimes united to increase their strength and wealth, and in so doing, developing cultures were merged and more sophisticated cultures established.

Nations eventually were formed and geographical boundaries set which included homogeneous groups of people. The setting of these boundaries often further unified the people, giving them a sense of brotherhood and oneness.

Wars were fought, which frequently resulted in one group being enslaved by the other. Entire peasant populations were enslaved; they were subjected as a group, with their families intact. It was recognized by both conqueror and conquered that this was a temporary arrangement—that in human terms the slave was the equal of his master. The slave had only been unfortunate enough to be on the losing side of a war.

This system of slavery was practiced in Greece, when Athens and Sparta were at their height. Even later, when Europe began to emerge into the nations we know today, wars continued to divide the people. But the warriors still viewed each other as equals—opponents in a battle for temporary supremacy.

By the eighteenth century, nationalism had become the primary force behind European thought and action. Individual Europeans, as well as groups, set priorities in terms of national interest. Devotion to one's homeland was considered a prerequisite for manhood. Respect for one's native language and customs was considered necessary for human value. It was generally accepted that men would be educated in their native tongues and that they would be taught to venerate the religions and cultures of their forefathers.

The principles of nationalism established codes by which international relations could be conducted. They established a system of unwritten international laws. Nevertheless, as European nationalism was becoming firmly institutionalized, European nations began colonizing Africa and Asia— disregarding all the principles and protections of nationalism in dealing with people who were not white. The European colonizers ruthlessly subjugated the Africans and Asians, exploiting the resources of the land as well as the labor of the people.

When the Europeans began their colonial expansion, they took the Christian gospel with them. Christianity played a dual role in the historical development of the eighteenth and nineteenth centuries. The church supported nationalism in Europe, but viewed non-Europeans as pagans—infidels who had to be saved by Christianity. The Europeans used their religion as a justification for their persecution and exploitation of other lands and peoples.

They interpreted biblical passages and religious lore to justify their hatred of darker people. Most frequently they referred to the story of Ham, which contended that Ham, the son of Noah, was banished to the south for disrespect to his faith. Today white racists are still quoting that story, asserting that the descendants of Ham, the banished, are the Black children of Africa.

The white Europeans quoted from the *Song of Solomon*, Chapter I, to assert the superiority of white beauty: "I am black, but comely, O ye daughters of Jerusalem, as the tents of Kedar, as the curtains of Solomon. Look not upon me, because I am black, because the sun hath looked upon me: my mother's children were angry with me: They made me the keeper of the vineyards, but mine own vineyard have I not kept."

By rationalizing that the Africans were heathens who must be converted, a way was found to superimpose the colonizers' mode of life on unwilling subjects. In a papal bull, in 1443, the Vatican granted to Portugal the sanctity to enslave all Africans, rationalizing that Blacks were pagans.

The Europeans had adapted the Christian religion and tailored it to their own needs. In each country religious worship had a distinctly national character. Customs and folklore were merged with religious teachings, resulting in new and distinct traditions. The western Europeans had adopted a Semitic Christ, but they envisioned him in their own image —with blond hair, fair skin, small nose, and blue eyes.

Missionaries as well as soldiers and merchants journeyed to Africa and Asia, but they did not grant the Africans the opportunity to adapt Christianity to their needs. The Africans were forced to swallow Christianity whole. Jesus, Mary, Joseph—by implication, even God—were white. The

Africans were not permitted to portray God as Black, or openly to incorporate the ceremonies of their forefathers in their Christian religious worship. The Europeans used both guns and torture to enforce their will, although the Africans and Asians fought fiercely in defense of their homelands and traditions.

The immigration to the New World occurred during the time of England's expansion and consolidation of her world empire, during the time that Britain's oppression of non-whites was most wholeheartedly accepted by Europeans. When European settlers first ventured to America, they sought to escape religious oppression and political tyranny in their native lands; they wanted to be free. These settlers, however, had been tainted by the racism of Europe and they brought with them the concept of white supremacy. Although they had come to America to escape classification determined by nobility of birth or inherited wealth, they took some of these loathsome values with them. Therefore, their thoughts about freedom and liberty remained restricted to their own kind.

The ideas of the settlers regarding Black Men were already quite well developed before they left their homelands. The culture and literature of Europe, especially England, perpetuated the ideas of white supremacy and prevented most Europeans from thinking in terms of justice and equality for all men. All Europeans accepted their right to suppress colored peoples in Africa and Asia and to exploit the resources of their lands. The determining factor in their treatment of colonial peoples was color. Geographical location was only a minor consideration.

When Columbus arrived in the New World, he was in search of a shorter route to the Far East; he was looking for a way to expand further the riches of Europe. He found

America, a vast rich land already inhabited, but inhabited by nonwhites—a fact that prompted him to write to the Queen of Spain that there were immeasurable riches in the land he had discovered and that the natives were remarkably well suited for slavery.

European disregard for the rights of nonwhite people was imported to America with the first boatload of white explorers. When Europeans began to settle in the New World, they exhibited the same attitudes toward the Indians that other Europeans had exhibited toward the Africans. In fact, these settlers had rather curious ideas about Indians. They seemed to feel it was the Indians who were the interlopers, that white men had finally arrived to claim what was rightfully theirs. They judged the Indians as "savages" and "animals" and proceeded to deal with them on that basis.

The Indians were cheated and dispossessed, at times tortured and killed. Many treaties and agreements were made between the whites and the Indians. In every case, white men broke the treaties, taking the land, pushing the Indians farther and farther west—eventually relegating the few surviving red men to reservations.

The American settlers adopted the European form of nationalism to fit the American situation. All the guarantees of European nationalism were included in the American variety, which continued to develop among the settlers. Eventually the loyalty of many of the settlers to their motherlands was completely transposed to their new country. They became Americans.

The Black Africans who were being shipped from Africa to America as slaves were not included under the protections of American nationalism. As a result of necessity, the slaves developed a unique form of nationalism of their own. It was not easily defined or neatly determined. It could not have been; the slaves were systematically divested of all of the trappings of their native African nationalism. In place of the African nationalism that could not be preserved came a solidarity of purpose among the first American slaves. The slaves developed a true "Black" Nationalism, a unity based on Blackness rather than tribal origin or former status.

In addition to bringing racist attitudes, the European immigrants also planted the roots of capitalism in America's land. It was generally true that the Europeans who came to America represented Europe's lower economic class—they were frequently rejects of European capitalism. Some were adventuresome and spirited; others were criminals; few were "successful" as judged by the standards of the Continent. But they did not come to America to destroy capitalism. They did not cross an ocean to find a better way of life. They crossed the Atlantic to extend the old way. Their desire was not to make a better world but to get a better piece of it. It was a selfish quest, for they sought richer opportunity. They wanted to reach the top of the economic ladder; they imported Blacks to occupy the lowest rung.

With this psychological and economic background, it was not difficult for the new American settlers to accept the concept of human slavery. It was not repugnant to them because the culture they brought was not founded on moral precepts. No doubt the whites relished their role as masters. Even the non-slaveholders, the majority of the early Americans who were not wealthy enough to own slaves, could identify with the white masters and could find comfort in the fact that they were more like the masters than like the slaves. After all, they were white. It was solely a matter of economics whether or not one owned slaves—no question of morality was involved.

White Americans then, as now, viewed the world through white eyes. They interpreted historical and current events on the basis of their own experience. They saw an America of opportunity, an America that was good to them. Seldom did they realize that Black Men saw America through Black eyes; the picture was literally and figuratively much darker.

Blacks were brutally herded here, separated from family and friends, unaware of what to expect, unable to change their destinies. Uprisings were frequent during those days. Insurance companies were just being formed, but the slave ships could not be insured because the "risk" of insurrection was too great. Shipmasters were aware of this and used oppressive methods to break the will and physical resistance of the slaves. Blacks died in the jungles. Blacks died on ships. Blacks died from disease and whippings. It is said that the route taken by the slave ships in the deathly journey from Africa to America is strewn with the bones of Black Men who—were they the fortunate ones?—did not make it.

Slaves had to adapt in order to survive; their adjustment was focused on the perverse mentality of the white racists. They survived by cunning, wit, compromise, and deceit. They rose in rebellion when possible and lay in wait when necessary.

Only about one-third of the Africans captured and sold into slavery reached the New World alive. When they reached America, many more died trying to escape. Some escaped and ran into the wilderness, where they often found other runaways and set up camps and settlements. These former slaves, who became known as Maroons, frequently joined with Indian tribes, living and working with the Indians.

Such instances were particularly numerous in the West Indies. In the early days of the slave trade, most African slaves were taken first to the Indies, then transported to the United States. At that time the slave traders were not as well organized as they would soon become. It was somewhat easier for the slaves to escape at these stopovers than it was when they reached America's southern states.

In spite of the fact that members of the same tribes were carefully kept away from one another by the slave traders to prevent communication and possible conspiracy, the runaway slaves retained a remarkable amount of their African culture.

Those slaves who were transported to the United States did not give up fighting. In spite of the increased security measures taken by slaveholders on the continent, the slaves, with the help of a few white abolitionists, established the legendary Underground Railroad that aided thousands of slaves yearly to escape to freedom.

During the years of slavery, as well as the years following, there were individual Black leaders who strongly influenced the history of their people. It was through the tireless effort of these Black men and women, who somehow retained their dignity and sense of purpose in a world of cruelty and degradation, that Black Americans were afforded a chance for survival.

In the early days of slavery the slaves produced almost no literature of their own. The slaveholders astutely realized that education and knowledge would strengthen the natural desire of the slaves to be free and make them potentially dangerous. By law the masters were subject to imprisonment for teaching a slave to read and write.

According to a North Carolina statute passed by the general assembly of 1830–31, which was fairly typical:

. . . any free person who shall hereafter teach or attempt to teach any slave within the state to read or write, the use of figures excepted, or shall give or sell to such slave or slaves any books or pamphlets . . . shall, at the discretion of the court, if a white man or women, be fined not less than $100 (one-hundred dollars) or more than $200 (two-hundred dollars) or imprisoned; and if a free person of color, shall be fined, imprisoned or whipped, at the discretion of the court, not exceeding 39 (thirty-nine) lashes, not less than 20 (twenty) lashes . . .

The penalty for any slave who taught another slave to read or write was "39 (thirty-nine) lashes on his or her bare back." The wide discrepancy in punishment set for Black and white for similar crimes was typical of the laws of that period. Almost invariably the mode of punishment for slaves was exclusively physical. Fines against the slaves would be meaningless as they almost never had money, and imprisonment of the slave would prove costly to the owner—who would surely be unwilling to release a slave from working in the fields or the "big house." Thus the use of the whip and the lash were reserved almost exclusively to Black Men.

The slaveholders also realized that an effective safeguard against massive uprisings was the vague promise of a way out—one day—maybe. The possibility that the slaves might buy their freedom inspired many to continue working even though the dream of freedom was not likely to be fulfilled. They could find comfort that once, in another county or even in their own county, some old slave had bought his freedom from his master. If he could do it, maybe they could, too. At times these nebulous hopes were all the slaves had to keep them alive.

Some slaves did manage to buy their freedom, while others escaped to the North. The slaveholders frequently posted rewards and offered bounties for the return of runaway slaves. Advertisements were placed in northern newspapers describing individual runaways and offering rewards for their return.

It was not uncommon practice for slaveholders to scout free states for Black Men who could be "framed" for slavery. In court southern slaveholders identified Black Men as runaway slaves whether or not they were in fact. Rarely did the court rule for the Black defendant. In most cases it was the word of a Black Man against a white man, and in a racist judiciary the white man wins. The Fugitive Slave Law and the laws of evidence prevented a Black Man's word from being accepted as evidence in court.

In spite of these tricks and devices, some slaves did stay free. Some of these freedmen could read and write, and a literature of Black America began to develop. This literature was generally influential in strengthening the bonds of nationalism among the Blacks. The writings of such men as David Walker, a militant Black preacher, inspired many Black men and women who would become leaders of their people.

One of the first and most influential pieces of this literature was a pamphlet that appeared in 1829 entitled *David Walker's Appeal in Four Articles: together with A Preamble, To the Coloured Citizens Of The World, but in particular and very expressly to those of The United States Of America.*

Fear not the number and education of our enemies against whom we shall have to contend for our lawful rights guaranteed to us by our makers; for why should we be afraid when God is and will continue to be on our side?

The above quotation from *Walker's Appeal* is indicative that at least some Black Christians were applying their religion to meet their needs. These men might still be preaching on behalf of a white Jesus, but their Jesus was just and their faith led them, like the Hebrews of the Old Testament, "to take up arms in defense of righteousness."

Of course, many Black preachers spoke for Christianity because it was the only way they could meet with their people unobserved by the master. Usually they met on the grounds of the plantations in crude chapels composed of brush and trees that were bent and tied to form arbors— hence the term "brush arbor" preachers. Militant Blacks had little hope of communicating with other slaves unless they did so through religious preachings—the overseers were highly vigilant.

Inevitably the plantation owners realized that religious meetings and services were being used to plan escapes and plot rebellions. Laws were passed that slaves could hold no meetings unattended by at least one armed white man—and the overseer became omnipresent.

After the rebellion led by Nat Turner, Black People were not permitted by law to hold any regular worship services, day or night. Slave owners could take slaves to their own services (hardly a common practice) or the slaves would have to do without religious inspiration. The white slave-holders sometimes used the device of forcing their Negro agents to become preachers, thereby providing a resource of intelligence information on the activities of their slaves and maintaining control over the slaves through some of their own people. These treacherous preachers were given the greatest rewards by the white masters with a view to establishing conservatism and restraint in the Black Church.

Writing such as David Walker's was suppressed by the existing establishment. Copies of Walker's writings could not be sold or passed openly among the slaves. However, it was no more possible then than now to suppress ideas completely, to control completely the expression of free thought. Legal censorship was no more effective in the days of slavery than today. Walker's writing received wide clandestine distribution among the slaves and was no doubt deeply influential in keeping Black Nationalism alive.

It is somewhat surprising that the only man praised by Walker in his writing was Richard Allen, founder and first bishop of the African Methodist Episcopal Church in America, which started out in Philadelphia in the 1780's. Walker's praise was surprising because Allen did not advocate slave violence in the pursuit of freedom. But Allen earned Walker's respect as well as the respect of other contemporary militants in many ways.

Although Allen originally belonged to the Methodist Church, his futile attempts to advance Black People within that structure convinced him of the need for an independent Black Church. Consequently Allen was primarily responsible for the first nationwide Organization of Black Americans, a structure and organization still in existence today. That this structure was religious in nature was indicative of the fact that any other form of organization would have been mercilessly smashed by the dominant whites. It was not equally indicative of any Black commitment to Christianity. It was largely through that first Black organization that any mass Black communication was accomplished. It was partly through the efforts begun by Bishop Allen that Black Men remembered their potential—and it was their knowledge of their own potential that gave them the courage to go on fighting.

During the long struggle to abolish slavery, there was much debate regarding the wisdom of violence by slaves and their abolitionist supporters. The debate was remarkably like the debate still raging today in and around our nation's ghettos regarding the advisability of violence by Black Men in their quest for racial justice and freedom. While the intellectuals and theorists argue, Black Men are forced to deal with the facts of daily oppression and prepare for confrontation—if necessary, violent confrontation. It is often the men who do not have to live in degradation—those white men who have never had to confront oppression except in theory and those Black Men who have, because of some special circumstances, been isolated from their people—who are most likely to advocate nonviolence, patience, and continued fortitude.

While others debated the wisdom of violent slave uprisings, Nat Turner, a young "brush arbor" preacher, organized one of the most extensive slave revolts. In 1831, Turner, beginning with a band of only six slaves, started a rebellion that was to attract and involve slaves from all over the county of Southampton, Virginia. Turner's conviction that God did not intend his people to live in injustice compelled him to lead his Brothers in rebellion.

Even in this strong commitment to his fight for freedom, Turner was not insensitive to human suffering and not inclined to wanton slaughter. According to the Richmond *Enquirer* of November 8, 1831, as quoted by Herbert Aptheker in his study of *American Negro Slave Revolts*, Turner was paraphrased as having said "indiscriminate slaughter was not their intention after they obtained a foothold, and was resorted to in the first instance to strike terror and alarm. Women and children would afterwards have been spared, and men, too, who ceased to resist." It was also significant that Turner and his men did not slay the poor whites, who were subjected to so many of the indignities and humiliations visited upon the slaves themselves. Their wrath was reserved for the oppressor—the men who had caused the intolerable conditions of slavery.

Perhaps inevitably—for the odds against Turner and his band were great—the rebellion ended in defeat. After months in hiding, Turner was captured, tried, and sentenced to hang. Nat Turner was executed on November 11, 1831— a martyr to the cause of his people.

The legacy of Nat Turner was one of courage and independence, of honor and hope. In death Turner became a part of the folklore of the South—an almost legendary hero, a symbol of the Black Man's courage and the Black Man's pride. Nat Turner's memory remained vivid in his home county and in his home states of North Carolina and Virginia, where Black People continued to revere his memory. Elsewhere, however, the facts of his rebellion were little known, and information regarding the rebellion was suppressed. Rarely, if ever, was his name mentioned in states across America, not even in schoolrooms where Black children were taught. Consequently, until fairly recently Black People were deprived of the inspiration of this great leader.

However, largely through the efforts of Lerone Bennett and Herbert Aptheker, the story of Nat Turner has become well known. Nat Turner lives again to inspire and console Black Militants, who may be forced to follow Turner's violent path.

Typically, white America has reacted to the renaissance of Black Nationalism and its glorification of Black heroes with dishonesty and treachery. William Styron, a white southerner, has written a widely read and highly publicized Pulitzer Prize–winning novel, *The Confessions of Nat Turner* (Random House, 1967). This novel is purportedly based on a pamphlet distributed throughout the nation following the insurrection that Turner led, a pamphlet detailing Turner's story and the story of the revolt. Styron has imaginatively elaborated upon that short pamphlet, defiling the memory of Turner by depicting him as a confused religious fanatic motivated to violence by an obsessive love for a white woman—as a man with homosexual tendencies and a cowardly bent.

Obviously similar desecration of a white hero would be greeted with national horror and outrage. If an author were to suggest, even in fictionalized form, that any of America's early patriots, for instance, George Washington, were so basely motivated, his work would be greeted not with a Pulitzer Prize, but universal scorn. In fact, white Americans do recoil from facing the facts about their Founding Fathers. George Washington was a slaveholder and reportedly fathered a number of Black children. Few history books and no major theatrical production has yet dealt openly with these facts.

In Great Britain, Rolf Hochhuth's play *Soldiers*, a fictionalization of Winston Churchill's role during World War II, was badly received. Hochhuth's play, although sympathetic to the burdens of leadership during war, suggested that Churchill was a conniver and murderer. The English were properly horrified and rallied to the defense of their former prime minister, acting in a manner that would surely be emulated in America under comparable circumstances.

It is indeed significant and indicative of the popular American psyche that white America has greeted the publication of *The Confessions of Nat Turner* with such enthusiasm. I would never approve censorship and fully support the right of Styron to author such a book, but it is the wide acceptance of his theories by white Americans that is so symptomatic of American racism.

While abolitionist pressure in the North was greatest, just prior to the Civil War, Frederick Douglass, a former slave, was catapulted into national prominence. Douglass, an articulate spokesman, campaigned to arouse support among whites for the abolitionist cause. During the period when he was most closely associated with William Lloyd Garrison, the white abolitionist, Douglass advocated the nonviolent protest against slavery, although he had never been committed to nonviolence as a way of life. By 1847 he had become convinced that slavery could end in no other way than by bloodshed.

In his autobiography, *The Life and Times of Frederick Douglass,* he said:

Speaking at an antislavery convention in Selma, Ohio, I expressed this apprehension that slavery could only be destroyed by bloodshed, when I was suddenly and sharply interrupted by my good old friend, Sojourner Truth with the question, "Frederick, is God dead?" "No," I answered, "and because God is not dead, slavery can only end in blood." My quaint old sister was of the Garrison school of non-resistants, and was shocked at my sanguinary doctrine, but she too became an advocate of the sword, when the war for the maintenance of the Union was declared.

During this period, there were other Black Men, less well known than Douglass, who worked and agitated for the abolition of slavery as well as for national pride for Black Americans. Such a man was Henry Highland Garnet, a Black minister and contemporary of Frederick Douglass. Garnet, an early advocate of Black Power, was influential in educating Douglass to the realities of his time and converting Douglass to the advocacy of violent rebellion when necessary. Garnet believed that unjust laws—as exemplified in the Fugitive Slave Laws—should be resisted furiously and that slavery would not and could not end until the slaves themselves openly and violently challenged their masters.

The Reconstruction period following the Civil War was brief. For a few short years Black Men participated in government, but at no time were they allowed to enter the economy. After the Reconstruction came the terrible period of the Black Codes and the Ku Klux Klan. W. E. B. DuBois noted in *Black Reconstruction:*

It must be remembered and never forgotten that the civil war in the South which overthrew Reconstruction was a determined effort to reduce black labor as nearly as possible to a condition of unlimited exploitation and build a new class of capitalists on this foundation. . . .

The lawlessness in the South since the Civil War has varied in its phases. First, it was that kind of disregard for law which follows all war. Then, it became a labor war, an attempt on the part of improverished capitalists and landholders to force laborers to work on the capitalist's own terms. From this, it changed to a war between laborers, white and black men fighting for the same jobs. Afterward, the white laborer joined the white landholder and capitalist and beat the black laborer into subjection through secret organizations and the rise of new doctrine of race hatred.

During the ensuing years a number of Black Men vied for the leadership of their people. They vied to determine the methods by which Black People would seek their freedom.

Booker T. Washington was the white man's choice for Black leadership. He was one of the earliest "responsible Negro leaders." Washington's willingness to deal with white men on their own terms and his acceptance of a secondary role in American society as a goal for his people revealed his inadequacy as an example and pacesetter for Black People. It seemed that Washington, although committed to a distinct form of economic nationalism, had either been quite successfully brainwashed by the white structure or found it politic to subordinate his admiration for his people in the interest of attaining the most menial gains.

Washington's most famous speech presented in 1895 at the Atlanta Exposition thirty years after the end of slavery caused white America to hail him as a great leader and spokesman for Black People.

As we have proved our loyalty to you in the past, in nursing your children—watching by the sick-bed of your mothers and fathers, and often following them with tear dimmed eyes to their graves, so in the future, in our humble way, we shall stand by you with a devotion that no foreigner can approach, ready to lay down our lives, if need be, in defense of yours, interlacing our industrial, commercial, civil and religious life with yours in a way that shall make the interests of both races one. In all things that are purely social we can be as separate as the fingers, yet one as the hand in all things essential to mutual progress.

Washington's concept of equality was limited and his ambitions for his people muted. In the same speech, he said:

The wisest among my race understand that the agitation of questions of social equality is the extremist folly, and that of all the privileges that will come to us must be the result of severe struggle rather than of artificial forcing.

Understandably, Washington's statements greatly pleased white Americans, and, in return for his good behavior, they granted certain concrete benefits to him and his people. He founded and organized the National Negro Business League, which fostered economic Black Nationalism. The league has afforded many Black Men opportunities for economic advancement through small business and has helped foster group identity in the Black Community with such slogans as "Buy Black."

Not all of the results of that organization were beneficial, however, according to Fishel and Quarles in *The Negro American*:

The League emphasis rested on the accepted virtues of the 19th Century: honesty, self-reliance, hard work and thrift—at a time when reformers were beginning to plead for government aid in controlling aggressive monopoly, finance capitalism, exploitation of labor, and slums. In holding up the small businessman as a prototype, Washington and the League obscured from race vision some other legal means by which white businessmen forged ahead. With understandable pride, Negroes arose to tell of their own or their community's business success without fully comprehending that this kind of success, in white America, was already outdated.

While Rockefeller, Gould, Carnegie, and others were consolidating their vast fortunes by trampling small businesses, Booker T. Washington was exhorting his people to become small businessmen. The few Black Men who were successful in business could be doubly proud that they had overcome, to some extent at least, not only the confines of being Black in a racist society, but the economic tide of the nation as well.

Washington was also the founder and president of Tuskegee Institute in Tuskegee, Alabama, a school that made significant contributions to the industrial and general training of Black People. There is no doubt that Tuskegee has provided many young Black men and women with training and education (mainly training) that they would not have otherwise received.

Washington's educational philosophy and vision were somewhat limited. In 1912, while addressing a group of white southerners, he said, "We are trying to instill into the Negro mind that if education does not make the Negro humble, simple, and of service to the community, then it will not be encouraged."

Tuskegee was the only institution in America to keep records of lynchings of Black Men. No white institution cared enough to keep such a tally. This record has been invaluable in helping Black People understand the nature and scope of their oppressor. Nevertheless, the achievements Washington was able to attain with his accommodating attitudes seem small reward for selling at least part of his people's soul.

Fortunately there were other Black Men who would not allow Washington's brand of leadership to go unchallenged.

W. E. B. DuBois was one of these men. DuBois' most unique contribution to Black America was his scholarly rendition of Black history. His writings and teachings were priceless for the educational value they had in the Black Community. Many young Black men and women were inspired by DuBois' pride and confidence in his people. Many young Blacks were encouraged and elevated by his vision and knowledge. His contributions to the study of Black history as well as his thoughtful essays and compositions on issues relevant to Black People classify him as one of the foremost intellectual leaders of Black America and a primary force in the development of Black Nationalism and Black pride in America.

This was true even though during much of his life DuBois was an advocate of integration. His reason for advocating integration was different from the reasons of most liberal whites, however. He wanted Black People to take full advantage of all available education and training to use their skills to aid other Afro-Americans. To advance these goals and to agitate for full and equal rights, he helped found the Niagra Movement, the forerunner of the National Association for the Advancement of Colored People. The goals of that organization were eloquently stated in the Niagra Movement Address in July, 1905:

We believe that [Negro] American citizens should protest emphatically and continually against curtailment of their political rights. We believe in manhood suffrages; we believe that no man is so good, intelligent or wealthy as to be entrusted wholly with the welfare of his neighbor.

DuBois believed that every race was led by its "talented tenth" and that the approximate 10 percent of Black Americans who would lead their people should be thoroughly educated. His theory of the "talented tenth," at the time it was developed, gave strong momentum to young Black People who desired education. He may have been something of an intellectual elitist, but he applied his theories in ways he felt to be most beneficial to all of his people.

Men of America, the problem is plain by you. Here is a race transplanted through the criminal foolishness of your fathers. Whether you like it or not the millions are here, and here they will remain. If you do not lift them up then we will pull you down. . . . The Talented Tenth of the Negro race must be made leaders of thought and missionaries of culture among their people. No others can do this work and Negro colleges must train men for it. The Negro race, like all other races, is going to be saved by its exceptional men. The problem of education then among Negroes, must first of all deal with the Talented Tenth.

DuBois' theory (quoted here from his article "The Talented Tenth," which appeared in *The Negro American*, edited by Fischel and Quarles) did not take into account the perverting nature of American racism. He could not fully envision the problems faced by the talented tenth, even when they had acquired the education he so strongly wanted for them. DuBois believed for a time that it was possible for dedicated Black People to be educated by the system without becoming part of that system, that they could reap the benefits of America and apply their skills and knowledge in the aid of their people. It has not always worked that way. The American system has been sufficiently devious to structure the education of young Blacks so as to strip them of initiative and social consciousness instead of developing these qualities. Many middle-class Blacks have not applied their education to the advancement of their people, but have used it to try to wedge themselves into the white American system.

According to E. Franklin Frazier in his excellent study of middle-class Black Americans, *Black Bourgeoisie:*

It has turned out that Negro higher education has become devoted chiefly to the task of educating the Black bourgeoisie. . . . The present generation of Negro college students . . . do not wish to recall their past. As they ride to school in their automobiles, they prefer to think of the money which they will earn as professional and business men. For they have been taught that money will bring them justice and equality in American life, and they propose to get money.

Although DuBois' initial theory of education might seem to invest an overly generous amount of faith in the American system, his other views of this nation were clear and uncompromising. DuBois perceived, prior even to 1903, some of the dangers inherent in that system. In *The Souls of Black Folk*, he said, "To be a poor man is hard, but to be a poor race in a land of dollars is the very bottom of hardships." He also recognized the very real possibility of genocide of Blacks by white America. Although in his day it was not conceivable that a "civilized" country could, by automation, wipe out millions of people at once, he said in 1903, "If worse come to worst, can the moral fibre of this country survive the slow throttling and murder of nine millions of men?"

DuBois' influence on subsequent generations of Blacks was incalculable. In *The Fire Next Time*, James Baldwin echoed DuBois' warning of the murderous nature of racism:

The glorification of one race and the consequent debasement of another—or others—always has been and always will be a recipe for murder. There is no way around this. If one is permitted to treat any group of people with special disfavor because of their race or the color of their skin, there is no limit to what one will force them to endure and since the entire race has been mysteriously indicted, no reason not to destroy it, root and branch.

W. E. B. DuBois was an activist. He believed, particularly in his later years, that definite action must be taken—that truth and knowledge alone could not free the Black Man. It was in this conviction that he became the first Black board member of the National Association for the Advancement of Colored People, then one of the most radical and forceful groups working on behalf of the Black Community.

As a young idealist he had believed that racism was the result of ignorance—that proper education could change the minds of whites. After years of bitter experience, he became convinced that white America was motivated not only by ignorance but by economics and that the economic interests of the elite caused them to encourage this ignorance of the masses.

In later years, thoroughly disillusioned by the American system, DuBois turned to Marxism. He went to Africa and spent the last years of his life in Ghana, a land in which one of the world's great civilizations, the Ghana Dynasty, had once flourished. During DuBois' entire life, he feuded bitterly with Booker T. Washington. DuBois' conviction that his people's learning capacity was at least as great as that of white men led him to repudiate Washington's leadership. This feud served to bring issues to the attention of the Black Community that might not otherwise have been discussed and provided insights that might not otherwise have been made.

At the same time that Washington and DuBois were exerting their influence in the Black Communities, Marcus Garvey, one of the most outspoken, dynamic, and dedicated Black Nationalists in America, accomplished what no other Black Man had done up to his time. He brought millions of Black Americans together in a cohesive organization—the first such organization not of a primarily religious nature.

Garvey was descended from the Maroons in Jamaica, the West Indies, and raised in the traditions of his people. Garvey's movement was dedicated to the eventual return of Black Americans to Africa. His movement reaffirmed the ties between Black Americans and their African brothers and provided a Black-oriented goal—a promised land—to which Afro-Americans could aspire. Rather than working and saving for limited objectives in America, Garveyites could strive to aid and eventually to join their brothers in Africa. In this respect, Garvey's movement was similar to the Zionist movement of the American Jews. Not all American Zionists have moved to Israel, but those who stay in America continue to offer support and encouragement to those who do make the move.

The objectives of Garvey's Universal Negro Improvement Association were responsive to the desires of Black People:

To establish a Universal Confraternity among the race; to promote the spirit of pride and love; to reclaim the fallen; to administer to and assist the needy; to assist in civilizing the backward tribes of Africa; to establish Commissionaries of Agencies in the principal countries of the world for the protection of all Negroes, irrespective of nationality, to promote a conscientious spiritual worship among the native tribes of Africa; to strengthen the imperialism of independent African States; to establish Universities, Colleges and Secondary Schools for the further education and culture of the boys and girls of the race; to conduct a world-wide commercial and industrial intercourse.

Garvey was an unabashed capitalist who endeavored to advance his people through business and free enterprise. In this sense, his program was similar to Booker T. Washington's, but Garvey's added ingredient, of which Washington's philosophy was severely lacking, was race pride.

Garvey's appeal to the Black masses had potency and force because he responded to the deepest need of any oppressed people—the need for independence. Although he did not die wealthy and although the UNIA ended in financial failure, his contributions to Black pride and cohesiveness were great. Marcus Garvey proved that Black People truly sought organizations that related to them as a group—not organizations manipulated and controlled by the white establishment. His movement provided evidence that when organizations are directly responsive to the Black Community, they will receive support and loyalty. His personal popularity and the loyalty of his followers demonstrated that Black People will follow those leaders who are directly responsible to Black constituents. The UNIA has provided, in many ways, an excellent model for all Black organizations to follow, making necessary adaptations to the tenor and reality of their own times.

Garvey, like Washington, had strong disagreements with DuBois, who contended that for the majority of Black Americans the dream of return to Africa was unrealistic and impracticable. The feud between these two men was well publicized by the white press, but although Garvey and Du-Bois often disagreed and were believed to be bitter enemies, Kwame Nkrumah at the All-Africa People's Conference of 1958 stated the ultimate truth—that the ideas and methods of these two men differed greatly, but that their goals were fundamentally alike. On that occasion, Nkrumah hailed both men as the pioneers who had "fought for American national and racial equality."

Today, as in the time of Garvey, Washington, and Du-Bois, there are Black leaders who seek to aid their people in divergent ways. Each makes his own unique contributions —more important, each represents a constituency, and each must be heard and respected. One of the most powerful and important of these constituencies in Black American life is the Nation of Islam.

The Honorable Elijah Muhammad, leader of the Nation of Islam, is spiritual leader to millions of Black Americans. He directs a religious movement with great implications and meaning for Black Men, not only in America, but all over the world.

Ever since becoming a potent force in Black American life, the Nation of Islam has been attacked and vilified by the white American press and even by moderate Negroes, for the impact of Elijah Muhammad and his teachings has affected far more Black People than just those who are believers in the Muslim faith. The teachings of Black pride and race consciousness have had a therapeutic affect on many young Blacks. The impact of those teachings have been felt in every Black organization—civil rights, religious, and social. The debate that has raged about the Muslims and their glorification of their own Blackness has been healthy and has inspired many Black People to re-evaluate their own positions and their own beliefs.

The followers of the Nation of Islam have been organized in their present form only since 1931. From only a few dedicated Black People working and preaching in 1931, the Nation of Islam has grown to one of the most important forces in Black America. Muslims are deeply respected by many ghetto residents for their reputations for clean living and their records of curing and converting not only habitual criminals but long-time drug addicts. It is apparent that such cures would only be possible for men who had found—or been shown—their own value and self-worth.

The speed with which Mr. Muhammad's teachings gained influence within the ghettos of America appears even more impressive considering that the Nation of Islam has not been projected favorably, if at all, by the white American mass media. It seems even more astounding when one realizes that the leader of the Nation—Elijah Muhammad—is rarely mentioned by the American press. Only rarely is this religion discussed by the mass media—and then in the most scathing and derogatory terms.

The cause of the Muslims has been advanced, however, by two of the most prominent and admired Black Men of the twentieth century—Malcolm X and Muhammad Ali. Although Malcolm left the Muslims before his death, while a minister in that faith he brought their cause to the attention of America. Muhammad Ali, heavyweight champion of the world, who is deeply admired by millions of Black youngsters, has helped to focus the attention of Black America on the Nation of Islam. These two men have drawn the attention of the masses to one of the few, if not the only, Black-inspired, Black-developed, Black-led, and Black-supported institutions in America, gaining many adherents and supporters among Black Men for the Nation of Islam. But even before Malcolm and Muhammad Ali added their voices, that religion was an important presence in the ghettos.

The contribution of Malcolm X to Black America, while a Muslim minister and afterward, is great. He overcame the racism of the Midwest, where he lived as a boy, and the oppression and degradation of the ghetto, where he was a drug addict and hustler. Years later in his autobiography he wrote:

I believe that it would be almost impossible to find anywhere in America a black man who has lived further down in the mud of human society than I have; or a black man who has been any more ignorant than I have been; or a black man who has suffered more anguish during his life than I have. But it is only after the deepest darkness that the greatest light can come; it is only after extreme grief that the greatest joy can come; it is only after slavery and prison that the sweetest appreciation of freedom can come.

Malcolm X was converted to the Muslim faith and the teaching of Elijah Muhammad while in prison. For several years he was one of the most articulate and best-known ministers of the Nation of Islam. He preached and taught across America, organizing and crusading for the Muslims.

In 1963, Malcolm was suspended, or "silenced," by the Honorable Elijah Muhammad, reputedly because of a statement he made regarding the assassination of President John F. Kennedy. Malcolm had remarked that "the chickens had come home to roost." He contended that it was the violence inherent in American society that had killed its own President. Shortly thereafter Malcolm left the Nation of Islam and founded the Organization of Afro-American Unity, in which he continued to preach a doctrine of Black pride and Black Nationalism.

Malcolm's thinking had been drastically revised after a trip to Mecca, the Holy Land of the Islamic faith. When visiting the Holy Land, he wrote his followers a letter (later published in his *Autobiography*) that read, in part:

Never have I witnessed such sincere hospitality and the overwhelming spirit of true brotherhood as is practiced by people of all colors and races here in this Ancient Holy Land, the home of Abraham, Muhammad, and all the other prophets of the Holy Scriptures. For the past week, I have been utterly speechless and spellbound by the graciousness I see displayed all around me by people *of all colors.* . . .

America needs to understand Islam, because this is the one religion that erases from its society the race problem. Throughout my travels in the Muslim world, I have met, talked to, and even eaten with people who, in America, would have been considered "white" . . . but the "white" attitude was removed from their minds by the religion of Islam. I have never before seen *sincere* and *true* brotherhood practiced by all colors together, irrespective of their color. . . .

With racism plaguing America like an incurable cancer, the so-called "Christian" white American heart should be receptive to a proven solution to such a destructive problem. Perhaps it could be in time to save America from imminent disaster—the same destruction brought upon Germany by racism that eventually destroyed the Germans themselves.

Although Malcolm X continued to preach Black unity, he began to include the white radical in his plan and his vision. Malcolm had begun to bridge the gap—a communications gap between the Black Militant and the white radical—when he was shot to death in the Audubon Ballroom in Harlem. Malcolm was killed by Black Men, but many Black People who know the system and the ways of The Man refuse to accept the white man's explanation of Malcolm's death. Many Black People firmly believe that the white establishment—probably the CIA—was responsible for Malcolm's murder. For Malcolm X might have been the one Black Man who could unite the dissident revolutionary forces in America and make great strides toward a true Black liberation. As such, he was a threat to the unjust social order in the United States and a Black Man with which to be reckoned.

The positive response of Black youth to Malcolm was immediate and strong, because in time of crisis he heralded a new kind of Black leadership—a Black leader who would tell the truth, who would not deal with The Man for petty rewards, who would not placate The Man to enhance his own comfort. Malcolm fully understood the need for Black People in America to identify with oppressed nonwhite people all over the world, particularly in Black Africa. He understood. He taught. His vision of freedom extended far beyond the borders of the United States—far beyond the western hemisphere. His vision of freedom was world wide and his ideas and teachings have survived him. His ideals will be preserved and will inspire dedicated and militant Black youth. He is worthy of their admiration.

It might seem incongruous that the same Black youngsters who revere Malcolm X and Elijah Muhammad would also idolize Martin Luther King, but they saw in Dr. King a man of ideals and commitment—a man of whom they could be proud. As a young man, the Rev. Dr. King successfully organized the Montgomery, Alabama, bus boycotts, signaling the start of the nonviolent movement for civil rights for Black People in America. Although the Congress of Racial Equality (CORE), under the courageous leadership of James Farmer, had already begun a nonviolent, direct-action drive for racial justice, it was Dr. King's boycott that captured the imagination of radical whites and some militant Blacks and set the stage for more than a decade of American history.

As founder and president of the Southern Christian Leadership Conference, Dr. King became the principal leader and spokesman for the nonviolent movement. His charisma and eloquence helped make him a symbol to Americans of goodwill—both Black and white. It is ironic that his own land never bestowed great honors upon him. In America he was subjected to the humiliation of jail after jail. It was Sweden, a foreign nation, that gave him his greatest formal honor—the Nobel Peace Prize.

Dr. King's whole way of life, his belief in peace and nonviolence, would not allow him to advocate Black Power. It would not permit him to think in terms of power or force. But he did adopt some of the precepts of Black Nationalism as advocated by the Black Power organizations. The slogan, "Black is Beautiful and It is So Beautiful to be Black," was adopted by the convention of the Southern Christian Leadership Conference during the last year of Dr. King's life.

Martin Luther King displayed a growing awareness of the impact of international issues on the lives of Black People in America. King strongly condemned the actions of his country in Vietnam. When he took his stand on issues of foreign policy and racism, many pseudo-liberal whites rejected his leadership. When he expanded his pacifism to include white America's actions in foreign lands, the man who had previously been admired as the rightful leader of Black America was suddenly criticized and attacked by the white press, as well as by the more "conservative" Negro leaders. He was condemned as a "traitor" and a "Communist" simply for asserting his constitutional right to freedom of speech. Nevertheless, he courageously articulated the mood of a large sector of the Black Community that opposed the war for a variety of reasons.

King followed other great Black leaders in his understanding of the international aspects of the nature of white oppression. DuBois, particularly in his later years, fully recognized the international scope of neo-colonialist oppression. The young Malcolm X was strongly influenced by the writing of DuBois and his appreciation of internationalism was strongly influenced by DuBois. King, in one sense at least, completed a historical cycle. DuBois' advocacy of internationalism won significant support within the Black intellectual community. More than thirty years later, Malcolm X taught the same principles, especially during the last few years of his life, spreading these principles among the Black masses as well as the Black intelligentsia. Dr. King, by adopting these principles, made internationalism respectable in the Black Community.

Although his intrusion into foreign policy discredited Dr. King as a civil-rights leader among many whites, it did not have the same effect among his Black supporters. Black admirers of Dr. King were more likely to investigate the true nature of American involvement in Vietnam, and, gaining understanding, they actively opposed the war.

The influence of Dr. King—in every aspect of American life—is incalculable. In *Before the Mayflower*, Lerone Bennett, Jr., stated:

He [King] built on the contributions of many men: W. E. DuBois, James Weldon Johnson, Walter White, Charles Houston, Eugene Kinckle Jones, Lester Granger, Thurgood Marshall, A. Phillip Randolph, Roy Wilkins, Mary McLeod Bethune and others—many others. . . . Above all, King had the help of impersonal socioeconomic forces: the continuing migration and the increasing political power of Negroes in the strategic industrial states of the North and West and the burgeoning Negro vote in the South; the power of money—the rise of the Negro middle class; the re-emergence of pride and a sense of roots and relatedness to the rising African states; and America's paradoxical position as a leader of "the free world" and a competitor in the Afro-Asian market place of ideas. These stones ground the movement. But, when all is said and done, they are still mere stones; the touch of an artist was required to give them life.

Martin King inspired and directed a movement that brought hope to America. That movement bought America a decade in which to change. The tragedy of Martin Luther King is that America did not change, did not respond to his call to conscience.

Dr. King's death brought more bitterness than perhaps any single event in recent Black history. Although most Black Americans did not share Dr. King's belief in nonviolence, they respected him and loved him. He was a man of courage and dedication. When he was slain by a white racist, Black America was reminded, more painfully than ever before, that for a Black Man to demand his dignity and assert his rights as a man is to endanger his life. Black America was again reminded that, for much of the white population, "the only good nigger is a dead nigger." If Martin Luther King, apostle of peace, could be slaughtered, then not one Black Man in America is safe.

When Dr. King died, white America lost its best friend among Blacks. Many white Americans knew this. Even many of the racists who wanted to be rid of King because of his nuisance value knew instinctively that he had offered them a reprieve. He had offered them at least some measure of protection from the wrath of Black America. He offered a release for the frustrations of Black America, using methods that were relatively unthreatening to the white structure.

Nonviolent passive resistance requires a special kind of commitment. It is a commitment that allows a man to accept insult and injury without retaliation. To ask such control from Black People who have been humiliated and assaulted and murdered for hundreds of years is hardly just or feasible. An alternative must be found.

For every ten men willing to make such a nonviolent commitment, there must be more than five thousand who will defend themselves, who will defend their families, when attacked. Self-defense is natural and desirable. It is a constitutional right and a moral duty. Self-defense is *not* in conflict with nonviolence. "Color Morality" would have us believe that a Black Man must be consistently and forever non-violent—even in the face of the most flagrant abuse—or he is labeled "sick," "depraved," "anti-social."

Whether massive nonviolent civil disobedience is desirable or not, by the time enough people could be mobilized to dislocate a city such as New York nonviolently, thousands of others would have been so thoroughly frustrated as to strike out violently. In order to make civil disobedience work on a large scale, thousands of people would be needed to block essential services—to block traffic and keep it blocked. As usual, in such a demonstration it would be the innocent who would suffer.

It seems to be the cruel nature of our world that it is always the innocent who suffer. In the case of armed revolt, so often it is the civilians, the children, the nonparticipants, who are wounded and killed. In the case of massive nonviolent disruption, if it could be organized, hospital services would be halted, police and firemen would be prevented from functioning. Again it would be the innocents, the children, the nonparticipants, who would suffer. At least in the case of armed rebellion the guilty would also suffer. The suffering of the innocents would not be doubly bitter, doubly futile.

Equally pertinent is the fact that nonviolence as a tactic could not be applied as successfully in the United States as it was in India. In India the demands were simple—the Indians wanted independence. They wanted the colonialist British to get out. There could be no question about when their goal was accomplished. The day independence was declared, the Indians had won.

The demands of Black Americans are not that simple. In India the British occupied foreign soil. They were greatly in the minority. It would have been the British who would have suffered most, even with their superior weaponry, should nonviolence have turned to violence. In America the odds are reversed.

In India it was less the power of the nonviolence than the threat of violence that defeated the British, who were fully aware of the existing dangers. They knew that if they remained too long, the massive demonstrations staged by Gandhi could not remain nonviolent. They knew that to avoid defeat in open warfare, they would be forced to withdraw.

Black People have been forced to live with white American violence since before the days of slavery. During slavery they could be subjected at their masters' whims to any form of mistreatment or violence. Following the Civil War, the Ku Klux Klan and southern sheriffs, as well as the average white citizens, felt free to vent their frustrations and inadequacies upon Black People. There have been four thousand lynchings of Black Men in the south since 1922. No doubt there were others unreported or undiscovered.

Black People today are subjected to the violence of the police, as well as to the violence of the war in Vietnam. They are subjected to the violence of hunger and poverty. They are subjected to the violence of the status quo.

American society is not founded upon nonviolence. There is little in the American heritage that is conducive to its teachings. The legends of the West, cowboys and Indians, and the American Revolution, Minutemen and Redcoats—America is rich with a history of violence. The classic means for problem solving in America is violence. Passivity and acquiescence are invariably interpreted as weakness.

American ingenuity has most often been directed toward the attainment of efficiency in violence. The repeater rifle was an American invention as were the Spencer and the Henry, which later became the Winchester rifle. It is hardly realistic to subject Black People to consistently violent abuse, in the meantime propagandizing the value of force—publicly equating violence with manliness—and then expect Black People to seek redress through nonviolent means.

It is remarkable that the era of nonviolent protest has lasted so long. If by some miracle, weapons—guns and bombs—were to disappear from the earth, human nature would demand that they be reinvented. In the meantime it is likely that if social conditions remained the same, men would attack one another with rocks and bottles, bricks, knives—even their bare hands. Only by addressing the divisive conditions—the huge economic differences and social inequities—can some sort of working agreement, some formula for coexistence, be found. For, in fact, coexistence is working nonviolence.

But coexistence cannot be achieved if only one side adopts the precepts. Only on a basis of mutual respect—and, if necessary, mutual fear—can such harmony be achieved. It is not yet possible to change human nature, but it is wise to deal with the realities of that nature. Man's instincts are still base. They are the same instincts that protected him in the untamed wilderness and that continue to protect him in an untamed world. When man is faced with a violent threat, his natural tendency is to strike back, to smash, beat, or kill. It is not likely that anything short of a miracle will change this reflex. The only solution to such a situation is so to structure society that men are only rarely faced with such situations on an individual basis and never on a group basis. Only such an agreement can be a basis for coexistence.

In rural America, where I lived for many years, most Black Men who are deacons have shotguns and rifles—one over the mantle and one over the door. They carry pistols and they administer Christian churches. Throughout the South, very few Black People live without weapons. When a boy becomes a man in the eyes of his father, he is taught how to use a gun and taught when to use it. It is the attitude of the owner of a weapon that determines its uses. The instrument itself is neither violent nor nonviolent. It is like time—neutral. It can hang on the wall or over the door and never be used. It can be used to kill a rabbit for food or it can be used to murder or to kill in self-defense. But the gun doesn't make the decision to be shot. Nor does the gun select the target.

So many southern Blacks own guns only because weapons are necessary for their self-protection. In many parts of the South they are also necessary for food. The relatively small investment in a shotgun can return many times its value in the amount of food it can provide for a poor southern family. Without guns they would be totally at the mercy of the southern sheriffs, as well as their lawless white neighbors —as personified by the Ku Klux Klan. In the North, too, guns are often necessary for self-protection.

My principal objection to federal gun-control laws is based on the manner in which they would surely be enforced. Gun-control laws would be strongly and consistently enforced in the ghettos and among Blacks in the rural South. It is hardly likely that they would be as conscientiously enforced in the suburbs of New Jersey or the middle-class white homes of Natchez, Mississippi. Such laws would be dishonest in the same way as the doctrine of "separate but equal." They would be passed although the reality of America would prevent their fair implementation.

Such laws would also be in direct conflict with the Second Amendment of the United States Constitution, which grants "the right to keep and bear arms." That amendment is not, as some modern pundits would have us believe, outdated or inapplicable to the present American situation. America's forefathers meant the words of the Declaration of Independence and sought to reinforce its principles in the Constitution. The Second Amendment gave force to the assertion of the Declaration of Independence that "all men are created equal. . . . That whenever any form of government becomes destructive of these ends, it is the right of the people to alter or to abolish it, and to institute new government . . . it is their right, it is their duty, to throw off such government, and to provide new guards for their future security."

It would hardly be a feasible program to "throw off such government" if absolutely all arms were controlled by the state. As it is, the state has machine guns, tanks, and heavy artillery, which are used unsparingly to suppress ghetto revolts.

If all guns, all power of physical force, are reserved to the government—the police, national guard, and army—the way to overt facism will have been cleared. The protection of arms, like nationalism, can work for justice only when applied to all people. When one group adheres to these principles, others must also, in defense of their own rights and interests.

The last hope that America's race problems could be solved by nonviolent means was represented by Martin Luther King. When he was murdered by a white assassin, the movement of nonviolent social protest died with him. But even during his lifetime, young Black Men were becoming more radical and less satisfied with the traditional interpretation of nonviolence. The Southern Christian Leadership Conference, as well as the early Congress of Racial Equality and the Student Nonviolent Coordinating Committee, had attracted young eager college students, many of whom were white, the remainder of whom were principally middle-class Blacks. As these youngsters picketed, demonstrated, sat-in, and marched, they realized that the changes they were demanding—and sometimes achieving—were insufficient to affect most Black People. They began to realize that the most fundamental changes would not be achieved through their nonviolent tactics. Even after Woolworth's and the corner drugstores were desegregated, the lives of most Blacks remained the same. Even after James Meredith became the first Black student to attend the University of

Mississippi, most of his people still attended segregated and inferior schools, still subjected to the same humiliations they had been subjected to all their lives.

During this period I worked closely with the movement, both as North Carolina State Youth Director of the NAACP and as National Chairman of CORE. As a lawyer, I handled thousands of demonstration cases and came into close and repeated contact with the young people who were the life-blood of the nonviolent movement. It was during this period that I helped organize the NAACP Youth Commandos— still the most militant branch of the NAACP.

In many cases, these young people, disillusioned by their lack of progress, became the most radical and revolutionary in the ensuing years. Because they saw their friends humili-ated and they suffered beatings at the hands of white cops, these young people would later foresake nonviolence for revolution. They tried to change America by offering them-selves as sacrifice, but learned that America was not inter-ested. Of course, many whites participated because the movement provided a diversion, an outlet for unrelated per-sonal rebelliousness. But many of them lost interest after the passage of the Civil Rights Act of 1964. They seemed to feel that their work had been done.

As a result of the relative ineffectiveness of the nonviolent movement and as a response to dashed hopes and mangled dreams, many Blacks and whites who had been honestly committed to achieving justice through nonviolent means turned to other leaders and other techniques. Failure by America to respond or even to communicate nonviolently convinced youth that nonviolence was futile. In 1966, at the Durham Convention of CORE, the organization officially changed its direction.

Emphasis was shifted from the more glamorous tactic of nonviolent, direct-action demonstrations to the more tedious, solid tactic of community organization for power. The press didn't pay much attention to this reorientation. But one year later, when the cry of Black Power became the marching chant of James Meredith's "March Against Fear," the press lost all perspective. Black Power and all it represented was descried as racist; CORE and SNCC were depicted as anti-white.

Black People—with the exception of such Negroes as Roy Wilkins, Whitney Young, and Bayard Rustin, who represent conservative constituencies—instinctively knew that Black Power was not racist but necessary, not anti-white but pro-Black. Many Black People within the NAACP and the Urban League supported Black Power and continued to work within those organizations to alter existing policies. The extent of the success of those who stayed in the Urban League can be measured by the fact that Whitney Young, in 1968, made many statements indicating support of Black Power. Other Black Power advocates within these organizations left to devote their energies to CORE and SNCC.

Stokely Carmichael, H. Rap Brown, and the young men who work with them are representative of young Black People in this country. They are directly responsible to the young Black radical community and they articulate the feelings and the needs of this very important group.

To understand the current mood of Black Americans, it is only necessary to review the history of Black People in this country. It is a history of slavery, disenfranchisement, degradation, and violence. Any man who understands that history could not be deceived by self-seeking "moderate" Negroes. If there is unflinching application of common sense and logic, even white men will have to admit that the conciliatory tone of the "moderates" could not be representative of a majority of Black People.

It must be recognized that there have been and still are powerful forces leading Black People toward the Black Power philosophy. The emergence of strong, independent Black nations in Africa has given great psychological impetus to Black Nationalism in America. Black children and adults now have a "homeland" of which to be proud. The disgraceful American anti-Black, anti-African propaganda exemplified by the Tarzan books and movies is no longer being believed. Black People can see on television and in the newspapers Black Men who are leading their own people to progress and independence. They see these leaders undermined and, as in the case of Patrice Lumumba, even killed by the white colonialists and their Negro henchmen. But it is no longer possible for Black Americans to believe the stereotypes created for them by white America. Black People are beginning to rediscover their heritage and to be proud of it.

It is difficult for Black as well as white America to decipher the truth from the garbled news they receive from the mass media. But Black People have one distinct advantage over white Americans. Black People know that they cannot trust the networks, the news services, or, in fact, almost any of the white press. They know enough to be skeptical of the character assassinations perpetrated by the American press against Black leaders around the world.

More and more, young Black People are going to the source; they are reading the works of such men as Kwame Nkrumah, former president of Ghana, now honorary president of Guinea. They are reading the writings of revolutionaries such as Ché Guevara, Regis Debray, and Frantz Fanon. Young Blacks are fast becoming radicalized. Many are becoming fully aware that the present system has not proven flexible enough to accommodate massive change, and they have learned the lessons of history.

This generation is reading Frederick Douglass and W. E. B. DuBois for the first time and finding their writings remarkably applicable today. DuBois' observations (in *Black Reconstruction*) are still highly pertinent:

In Africa, a black back runs red with the blood of the lash; in India, a brown girl is raped; in China, a coolie starves; in Alabama, seven darkies are more than lynched; while in London, the white limbs of a prostitute are hung with jewels and silk. Flames of jealous murder sweep the earth, while brains of little children smear the hills.

Young Blacks are seeing the dangers inherent in a system dependent upon racism. In the words of Frantz Fanon (*Toward the African Revolution*):

A society has race prejudice or it has not. There are no degrees of prejudice. One cannot say that a given country is racist but that lynchings or extermination camps are not to be found there. The truth is that all that and still other things exist on the horizon.

Fanon's realization echoes the admonitions of DuBois, Baldwin, and many others. But he developed his insight not as a result of racism in America but because of the racism of the French. His belief demonstrates even more strikingly the world-wide nature of oppression.

Young Blacks are also being educated about the devious methods of American colonialism, "semi-colonialism," and "neo-colonialism." Jean-Paul Sartre, in *Sartre on Cuba* (Ballantine Books, 1961), explains how the United States keeps Latin American countries dependent, especially citing the Cuban experience:

The regime of the one-crop system had given Cuba one of the most typical characteristics of "semi-colonialism": it forced all national activities to submit to dependence upon one sector of production controlled by the foreign power, directly linked to exploitation. The economy was completely conditioned by variations in the price of sugar in foreign markets; it could not direct itself and it remained at the mercy of a fall in price and values.

Young Americans are learning much from the experiences and philosophies of the Cuban revolutionaries. They are becoming aware that in other lands there are other methods of dealing with the historical problems of corruption and political treachery. In *Man and Socialism in Cuba* (Guaras-Book Institute, Havana, 1967), E. Ché Guevara wrote:

It is evident that there are dangers in the present circumstances. Not only that of dogmatism, not only that of the freezing up of relations with the masses in the midst of the great task; there also exists the danger of weakness in which it is possible to incur. If a man thinks that in order to devote his entire life to the revolution, he cannot be distracted by the worry that one of his children lacks a certain article, that the children's shoes are in a poor condition, that his family lacks some necessary item, with this reasoning, the seeds of future corruption are allowed to filter through.

In our case, we have maintained that our children must have, or lack, what the children of the ordinary citizen have or lack; our family must understand this and struggle for it. The revolution is made by man, but man must forge his revolutionary spirit from day to day.

Young Blacks are learning of revolutionary experiences around the world. They are becoming aware that the values of America need not be accepted—that treachery and oppression need not be tolerated. Inevitably, they are comparing the conditions and experiences of foreign revolutionaries to their own. And they are becoming convinced that their experiences are comparable in many ways to those of other oppressed people. Some are becoming convinced that in America, too, the only satisfactory answer is total revolution.

As white America continues to use every device to avoid true progress, Black America prepares for the inevitable. If America is to avoid open warfare, it must apply all of its devices and resources to developing a formula for racial coexistence instead of using those devices to maintain the status quo. If America is to avoid violent internal revolution, the white majority must acknowledge the validity of Black Nationalism in America. White America must recognize that within its boundaries exists a Black Nation and this nation must receive the same respect and honor accorded other nations.

Black People in the United States live in a state of *de facto* nationhood. We are a nation within a nation. The large majority of Black People live in landlocked islands of racial isolation throughout the United States. Black Americans speak a common language. They share cultural ties and a common history. Their dress, speech, music, and foods are similar. Their methods of dealing with white people, a prime factor of their culture, are similar. Their ability to deceive white people, born out of a necessity for survival, is the same. The racism to which they are subjected, whether they live in the North or the South, in Watts, Harlem, Atlanta, Durham, or Nashville, is of the same cruel intensity. The criteria for nationhood exists.

To see one of the communities in which Black People live is to see nearly all. Black People across America have responded to the conspiracy of white racism in ways very much alike. Today, as in slavery, they share the bonds of oppression and the bonds of race. Their destinies are forever linked by virtue of their color. The Black Nation of America is a fact. The only aspect of nationhood they lack is independence.

White America recoils in fear from acknowledging the existence of a nation within a nation, although white men, too, know of its existence. They fear the strength of a united Black populace. Their fear is based upon guilt. It is a realistic fear.

Every time a white American sees a Black Man, he witnesses the guilt of his forefathers. He witnesses his own guilt, too, and is reminded of his own responsibility for the perpetuation of that guilt. White men know—although they rarely admit—that Black People would be justified in any means they adopted to end their oppression. White men know that their own reaction to a violent Black revolution would be vicious and uncompromising. They know that they would respond to force with murder, torture, and even total genocide. Yet they refuse to take the steps to avoid such holocaust.

Perhaps their continued persecution of Black People, even in the face of world revolution, is a natural extension of the decadence of their own culture. Perhaps it is the consequence of a perverse death wish. Surely it is self-destructive in the face of massive evidence that violent revolution is beginning and growing all over the world.

It is possible that white America actually anticipates its own destruction—that the violent tenor of American society creates a suicidal pathology in the white majority. The conscious and unflinching choice of continued oppression indicates crippling shortsightedness, disregard for the children of the future, and an unconscious desire to indulge in a blood bath—even though much of the blood spilt would be white. It suggests a necrophilous society—a society obsessed with death.

146

In his essay "Creators or Destroyers?" psychologist Erich Fromm describes some characteristics of necrophiles:

The necrophilous dwell in the past, never in the future. Their feelings are essentially sentimental, that is, they nurse the memory of feelings which they had yesterday—or believe that they had. They are cold, distant devotees of "law and order."

Surely Fromm describes symptoms abundantly evident in white America.

This realization is particularly ominous because it establishes that for America to change direction, the society in general, as well as the powerful individuals who manipulate the society, must first recognize and then overcome not only their racism but other deep-seated pathologies that reinforce that racism.

White America must re-evaluate its motives and, even when it is most painful, accept the truth. Such re-evaluation would most certainly lead to the development of a new national consciousness, although it would hardly be in character.

Each white man seems to have developed his own rationale for disavowing his responsibility for the Black Man's suffering. Each white man seems to have devised excuses and pseudo-explanations to justify the actions of his ancestors for the slavery and degradation of Black People. He cites exceptions and examples of "good" masters, "good" slaveholders —a conflict in terms. There could be no "good" slaveholders.

Such rationalizations are unimportant to Black People. What is important is what white men have done. What is important is what those white people who claim to be "of goodwill" have not done. For in America, as in Nazi Germany, the only men without guilt are those who have actively opposed evil. Men like John Brown are exempt from the guilt of their people. For John Brown did as much in defense of Black Men as he would have done in his own defense. His commitment to justice was real and undeniable.

Every white man living today, whether he is Republican or Democrat, liberal or conservative, radical or reactionary, shares to some degree in the guilt of the nation. Only those white men who resist the political and economic re-enslavement of the Black Man as vehemently as if it were their own life at stake can be absolved. Black People can no longer allow white men to escape their responsibility to the Black Nation.

The twentieth-century American white man has attempted to re-enslave the Black Man and has, in effect, revived the status of "three-fifths of a man" for Blacks. The case of American Blacks against contemporary whites need no longer be based on the slavery imposed upon them by the founders of America. Those initial crimes laid the basis for modern crimes, but, more relevantly, it is against those white people, both in the North and South, who have joined in a conspiracy to re-enslave Black People in our time that our case is directed.

White Americans must reject excuses for their behavior and reject false theories that try to absolve them of their guilt. One such popular theory is that Black People are committing individual and mass suicide by participation in street rebellions—the so-called "riots." Actually, when Black People put their lives on the line by rebelling against an oppressive system, they are affirming their humanity. If Black People did not rebel, if they submitted meekly to oppression, then they would be committing suicide. Then they would be sacrificing their right to be free, autonomous human beings. They would be accepting for themselves and for their children a state of "living death."

Black People in America will not accept such status. Nonwhite people around the world will not accept such status. Only if white Americans painfully re-evaluate the policies of their nation, both foreign and domestic, might there still be time to achieve peace.

There are always alternatives open to the policy makers. They do not have to accept the precedents of the past when formulating national policy. It would have been possible, for instance, for America to deal very differently with Castro's Cuba. If America had not overreacted to the nationalization of industry by Castro, it would have been possible for the United States and Cuba to achieve a working alliance. By providing Castro's regime with economic aid when requested, by accepting the nationalization of American industry, the United States could have set an excellent precedent for all dealings with developing nations. Of course, many Americans would oppose such policies on the basis that the prestige of the United States would be undermined by negotiations on an equal basis with a tiny nation such as Cuba. But these critics fail to realize that there are many potential Cubas—in Latin America, Africa, and Asia—and that the combined forces of these nations could topple the awesome power of the United States. It would not even be necessary for these nations to unite formally. If threats to American power occurred all over the world, American forces would be too diffuse and weakened to maintain effectiveness. Ché Guevara recognized this in his message that was made public in April, 1967 (in *Ché Guevara Speaks*, Grove Press, 1967).

All this (Revolution in the Third World) continues to provoke repercussions inside the United States; it is going to arouse a factor that was attenuated in the days of the full vigor or imperialism—the class struggle inside its own territory.

How close and bright would the future appear if two, three Vietnams, flowered on the face of the globe, with their quota of death and immense tragedies, with their daily heroism, with their repeated blows against imperialism, obliging it to disperse its forces under the lash of the growing hate of the people of the world!

And if we were capable of uniting so as to give our blows greater solidity and certainty, so that the effectiveness of aid of all kinds to the people locked in combat was increased—how great the future would be, and how near!

Ché's observations and predictions were based upon the realities he knew. They were surely apt in light of recent and current United States foreign policy. But if that policy was voluntarily altered and the economic base shifted, there would be no need for the violent revolutions envisioned by Guevara. It may still happen in the manner Ché expected; in fact it is highly likely. But it need not be so.

If the United States adopted a practice of making peace with each emerging nation on a basis of mutual respect, America would achieve real security—not a tenuous security guarded by missiles and guns. Such a policy would meet the ultimate criteria for any foreign policy: it would be in the "national interest." Of course, such a policy would require unaccustomed foresightedness from America's diplomats and industrialists. It would require that certain industrial plants and short-range financial interests be relinquished in order to attain a more just and stable world community.

In most of the emerging nations of the world, America's lease is up. American industry built many of the plants in Africa, but these plants were built by the cheap labor of the Africans. They were built with the resources of the nation —and they were built to exploit those resources primarily for the economic benefit of American industry.

American industry has received far, far more from these nations than has ever been invested, and it is now time for Americans gratefully to add up their profits and, when bid, graciously depart. In some nations it might be possible to negotiate agreements whereby American industry continues to be involved in a country, while training indigenous people to take over that industry and paying fair amounts of tax money to the developing nations. But such agreements cannot be reached unless it is at the instigation of the indigenous populations. In most cases Americans would do best to withdraw.

The adoption of such policies would require basic changes within America. It would be necessary to socialize many aspects of the economy in order to become more self-sufficient. America cannot continue to be dependent upon the subjugation of the world's oppressed. Unless the economic base of the United States is radically altered, it will not be possible for America to develop intelligent, just policies in dealing with the people of the world. It will not be possible to free America and the rest of the world within the limitations of capitalism.

First, however, America must re-evaluate its own domestic policies. As long as oppression and degradation exist within America, it is unlikely that foreign policy will be revamped. America has the means to save itself. It has not yet demonstrated the will.

If white America accepts the challenge of the future, what steps could be taken to avoid otherwise inevitable internal conflict? What solutions and programs could be applied to alter the future?

Although the American government has the power, money, and resources to initiate programs of massive aid to the Black Community, the government, comprised of white

Americans, does not have the capacity to operate in a non-racist way. It does not have the capacity to administer justice to Black Men or set standards for Black People. Therefore, if change is to be made, the white government must relinquish some of its power, money, and resources to the Black Community—either collectively or individually—and allow that community to solve its problems. By the time such a gesture is made by the American government, a long step toward solving America's race problems and realizing the goal of racial coexistence will have been made.

The Black Community must be allowed to solve its own problems, but it must be provided with the resources to do so, resources earned but never collected—earned over years of toil and oppression.

The years of slavery and the subsequent years of disenfranchisement and poverty have entitled the Black Man to far more than welfare, far more than a guaranteed annual income. They have earned him respect and honor. They have earned him opportunity.

Although Black People form a nation and share a heritage and vision, there has never been and probably never will be unanimity among Black People on any given issue. This diversity of opinion is not restricted to Black People. It is characteristic of every thinking group of people. The expectation of white America that Black Americans should not have such differences is further evidence of white America's denial of the Black Man's basic humanity.

There is no one man or organization or philosophy that represents all Black People. At times Black People must unite behind one man or organization, if only temporarily, when that man or organization is under attack by the white establishment. Even many Black People who did not support the policies and actions of Adam Clayton Powell rallied to him when he was unjustly and arbitrarily expelled by the

House of Representatives. On other issues, however, Black People disagree. *If there is any one goal that is shared by all Blacks, that goal is self-determination.*

The complex problems of today cannot be solved by addressing the needs and desires of only one segment of the Black Community. The needs and desires of every major group must be met.

Probably about 10 percent of Black Americans are really interested in being integrated into the white society. That percentage would undoubtedly drop drastically if other feasible alternatives—such as participation in autonomous, all-Black communities—were available. At present, many middle-class Black People are faced with only two realistic alternatives—life in the ghetto, where living conditions are awful, and moving into white neighborhoods, where at least the material comforts are available. There are far too few Black neighborhoods for middle-class Black People and no Black communities that are independent of the surrounding white society. Therefore, more affluent Blacks must either live among poverty or admit dependence upon The Man.

If other alternatives were available, probably less than 4 percent of the Black population would choose to integrate with white America.

If white America is to make progress, the integrationists must be accommodated. The courts must strictly enforce laws against violation of the liberties and rights of Black Men—whether those Black Men are seeking integration or not. Black People must be free to choose. Their choice must be supported and enforced by the entire American structure. The white society must deal severely with every white individual, every white corporation that stands in the way of a Black Man seeking integration. Most Black People will surely choose to live among other Black People. But access to white America must be unhampered. As long as such access is barred, Black People will be assured that America is still racist.

The American government must also aid those American Black People who want to live and work in Africa. In many cases, the primary factor keeping Black People in this country is financial. Most Blacks do not have the money necessary to relocate in Africa—to pay for their transportation and allow them to settle down.

Many emerging Black nations cannot afford to take in any more unskilled laborers than they already have. Africa needs trained technicians, engineers and teachers, architects and doctors. African nations cannot afford to encourage Black Americans to migrate to African shores unless those Americans have skills and training needed to assist these developing countries.

The Congress of the United States should develop legislation to provide educational training to Black Americans that would be useful to them upon their return to Africa. Such training could be administered through existing colleges and universities as well as through schools with curricula developed particularly for this purpose. Such a program would promote goodwill with African nations and simultaneously help Black People to build a new and better life.

Manpower training is now done on a limited basis provided for by an act of Congress. With imagination and ingenuity, an act could be drafted to accommodate the objectives outlined here. Private funding could also assist in developing parts of the programs in the United States as well as in Africa, in cooperation with the African nations involved.

If America exerts all its influence within the United Nations to grant independence to the Black People of Southwest Africa, negotiations could begin to send American Garveyites to that territory to live and work. Such an arrangement would be beneficial both to the Africans, who need skilled technicians, and to the Garveyites, who would have an opportunity to help build and develop a new nation and become part of an emerging culture.

In order to press for such radical changes, the United States would have to end its substantial economic dependence upon countries such as South Africa. The United States now provides the margin on which the racist white government of South Africa survives. If America's economy is made viable, it will not be necessary to continue such investment. If increased socialism frees America from its most offensive commitments, the nation will also be free to make new and beneficial alliances.

The members of the Nation of Islam—the Muslims—seek land within the continental limits of the United States on which to establish an independent Black state. They believe that it is not possible to coexist with whites and they feel that Black People have earned land within the country of their Black forefathers. That such land has indeed been earned is indisputable. There can never be adequate compensation for the pain and bitterness of slavery. There can never be adequate compensation for the destructive effects America has brought upon the descendants of slaves. Such demands are not unprecedented. It was the Mormons who moved westward to establish the state of Utah, who created their own government, schools, and industries. Having done so, they were gobbled up and forced to become a state by a young America, already greedy.

Another precedent for this proposal is the land-grant colleges established during the early years of this country. As with the Demonstration Cities Act, new cities can be built with land the government now owns or could acquire, to be owned and controlled by Black People—with technical assistance coming from government and private industry.

There is plenty of land available in the United States that could be used for this purpose. Seventy percent of all Americans live in urban centers. The land space now occupied by the cities is only 0.7 percent of the total area of the United States. Adequate land could easily be provided on which the Muslims could settle. Revolutions have invariably been fought for the equitable redistribution of land, wealth, and power. America now has the opportunity to effect such a redistribution without accompanying bloodshed.

Many Black Americans have no desire to leave their communities. They simply want them to be livable. Under the present system they do not have the facilities to make them livable.

Ownership of the land area in places such as Harlem and Bedford Stuyvesant must be transferred to the residents, individually or collectively. One method for accomplishing these transferrals is to entrust them to community corporations, with trustees elected by the members of the Black Community. Existing governmental programs such as the Demonstration Cities' program, the Federal Housing Authority, and the Commerce Department program, along with contributions from private industry, must be coordinated to accomplish this end.

Ownership of businesses in the ghetto must be transferred to Black People, either individually or collectively. Possibly some of the present absentee owners can be retained by the government as technical advisers to the new owners.

Attached to this program can be the "communiversity" or other training agencies where Black People can be taught to operate various types of businesses. All government facilities in the ghetto must be run and operated by Black People —for instance, the post office, the judiciary, police department, welfare department, board of education, and all other such agencies. As technical assistance can be given to

Africa, technical assistance can be provided for Black Americans.

In all ghetto areas of the United States, Black universities must be established. These universities should be staffed and run by Blacks, with curricula concentrating on Black history, Black culture, and a collection of historical information pertinent to Black People.

This is not unprecedented. The Schomberg Collection now rests on 135th Street in Harlem—a tiny model for a great project. Even that tiny beginning is neglected by the New York Public Library, which is responsible for its maintenance.

These programs, if fully implemented, would solve many of the internal dilemmas facing the United States. In order to bring about popular white acceptance of such programs, the propaganda machine of the nation would have to be redirected. This would have to be done simultaneously with the introduction of some of these programs. There is not time to re-educate white America thoroughly before action on behalf of Black America is taken. There is no more time for presidential commissions and scholarly reports. These discourses and reports have merely been used as tactics and excuses for further delay.

There are two alternatives for America—two possibilities. The remedies for strife, internal as well as external, are clear. Either we are going to have a forced change, a bloody revolution, or we are going to have an enforced, legal, and orderly progress, one effected by men in power dispersing that power and re-creating a legal system that is supreme, equitable, and just. The Black Man in America must be accepted fully by the society; he must be granted his full constitutional rights and his just share of the power and wealth of America. There must be new policies for international relations. Black People will not be satisfied while their Black and colored brothers still suffer from colonialism and oppression.

In the words of John Killens, "We are not Genet's *Blacks*, waiting for the day we can assume the role the white man played for centuries" (from *Black Man's Burden*). We are instead the only conscience left in America. It is by the demands we place upon America that there is hope for justice. The continuation of present policies can inspire only disaster. As frustrations in the ghetto increase, there will be more and more rebellions, more and more violence. White America will respond, as always, with force. The patience of white men in dealing with nonwhites is notoriously short, and the great American experiment in social progress—the abortive "War on Poverty"—has ended.

White mayors will give orders to "shoot to kill" looters and arsonists, as Chicago's Mayor Daley has already done. America's governors will call for the national guard, giving the order to "shoot them down" and "stack them up," as has Governor Maddox of Georgia. These forces will surely be unhesitatingly supplied by a willing President, regardless of his party, with the rationale of containing "crime in the streets."

It is likely that the McCarran Act will be invoked against many Blacks, as well as radical whites, and when the maintenance of prison camps becomes too expensive, the wholesale execution of Blacks may begin. By that time the war psychosis would, as in Nazi Germany, stifle all protest. The demands of the war in Vietnam or other similar colonial wars and the threat of a faltering economy further endangered by a rebellious Black population may force America to choose between genocides.

If the current trend in political and economic thought prevails, the United States will act to annihilate one problem or the other. If there is only one colonial war—one Vietnam —it is probable that tons more of bombs will be dropped and the peasant populations wiped out. However, if as Ché Guevara envisioned, there are many Vietnams—in Africa and Latin America as well as Southeast Asia—the most potent threat to the United States will be at home. The rebellions in the streets will divert troops, money, and guns away from the foreign fronts.

Warfare in America's cities would result in deaths on both sides. Young white guardsmen would be shot down as well as Black women and children. The whites would have the sophisticated weaponry but they would be restricted in its use because the battleground would be the American city —the American industrial centers. The Black Man would have the advantage of the guerrilla in any war—the advantage of surprise and elusiveness.

As mighty and as powerful as is America, it could not withstand the total onslaught of the oppressed. No economy is strong enough to support war on many fronts—and if the wars are fought against guerrillas, they are many times more costly. The result of such cataclysm would surely be the destruction of America, and with America's destruction, the rest of the capitalist world would fall.

I'd like to speculate what could be found in the mind and diary of a Black Man who might live through such terrible days. It is sometimes easier for people to understand what one individual endures than to comprehend the effect of social cataclysm upon millions. It is the nature of the human mind not to be able to really understand mass horror. Who of us can really comprehend the suffering of six million Jews? Who of us can really understand the suffering of millions of Black slaves? But who of us can fail to understand the suffering of a single child?

In view of this, I have tried to anticipate one possible nightmare in "Diary of a Black Man." The narrator, a man named William Richard Jones, tells a story of the possible future, perhaps fifteen, perhaps twenty years from now:

My family and I now await death at the home of a friend. We now await the inevitable onslaught from the American National Guard. We will die fighting. And we will die with the knowledge that our brothers will continue the fight and, eventually, win. I suppose that it is natural that at such a moment one reminisces. I suppose that it is unavoidable to relive mentally a period of your life that was the most decisive—the most fateful.

My personal conversion from "American Negro" to Black Revolutionary came about 1970, when the Congress adopted federal gun-control legislation. I had always had a gun. In the South, where I was raised, it was foolish and dangerous to be unarmed if you were Black. We hunted for food and protected ourselves from intruders. I had always accepted my right to do so as natural and unassailable.

After the gun-control legislation took effect, however, the police and national guard undertook a systematic attempt to disarm Black People. The precedent had been set in the late sixties during the rebellions in Plainfield, New Jersey, when national guardsmen, without warrants, stormed the homes of Black citizens and wantonly destroyed Black property while searching for arms. Then, with the advent of gun-control legislation, every time a minor racial disturbance occurred in a Black community, police took the opportunity to search Black People and their homes for arms, confiscating them and, often as not, jailing the owners.

For the first time I realized the power and evil inherent in this system. For the first time the full brunt of racist force was made to bear directly upon my life. For years, although I had been curtailed by the fact of my Blackness, I had operated under an illusion that I was living in an "open society." This belief both hampered me and helped me. It gave me the courage to continue struggling to "make something of myself," although the odds in this white system were high against me. But it also created a distrust and even hatred for many of my people. The schools and churches taught me I lived in a "free country." And I believed them. Why, then, I reasoned, had my people not advanced within this "free society"? Why had they not forced their way in among the power brokers? The reason, I concluded—although I never admitted it to myself or others—was that Black Men were inferior.

In 1970, however, after the cops had smashed into my home in Harlem, roughing up my wife and children and confiscating my property, my eyes began to open. I began to talk to the militants in my neighborhood—those men who were preaching open revolt against the white man's system. Their ideas made sense. And the questions they raised encouraged me to seek answers in books—books about Black Men that had not been included on my reading lists in the public schools.

I could no longer accept the degrading daily life forced upon me by this system. I could no longer watch my wife insulted and my children hurt. I could no longer deny my manhood.

By 1975 and the passage of the National Registration Act, which had first been suggested by HUAC in 1968, requiring all Black People to carry federal identification cards, I was already a member of an underground revolutionary cell. At that point my wife was still unaware of my involvement and, I think, a little ashamed of my lack of overt militance. I didn't want to tell her and make her afraid that I, like many of our friends—both innocent and guilty—would be caught and sent to one of the concentration camps provided for the McCarran Act. We had seen and heard of too many men being carried off, sometimes without charges, in the middle of the night.

For Black People the nightmare of Nazi-like tyranny was real, but for all but a few whites this oppression was considered a just and reasonable response to guerrilla warfare.

I was inspired by the courage of Black youth and the militancy of those young Blacks who refused openly to register, even sitting in on college campuses in protest. Of course, these kids were ruthlessly herded into camps for their trouble. But after that incident, which in view of the tight censorship was surprisingly well covered in the press, at least America could not claim ignorance.

My wife and I watched on television the President's speech calling for the passage of the National Heritage Act, an act that would declare subversive all overt expression of "alien" cultures. It was clear by the selective wording and tone of that speech that what the President really meant was Black culture or African culture. Betty, of course, was incensed and began vilifying me for my nonrevolutionary attitudes. I told the truth. She was proud and happy but afraid. From then on she, too, became an active revolutionary, smuggling arms and carrying messages.

It was about this time that the federal government announced the development of a so-called "pill bomb," a bomb no larger than an aspirin that could destroy limited areas, such as Harlem, without danger of fallout in surrounding areas. This information, instead of intimidating the guerrilla fighters, spurred them to bolder action. For we knew that time was short. If we didn't spread out and hit in as many industrial centers as possible, the government would not hesitate to use the pill. And if we escalated, there was always the danger of forcing his hand. It was a chance we had to take.

In Bedford-Stuyvesant, the government tested the pill. Blacks were allowed out of the doomed ghetto prior to bombing only if they would produce valid registration cards as well as provide the name of at least one Black subversive who would automatically be marked for execution. Many Blacks who did not know the guerrillas chose death rather than mark an innocent friend. Many others who did know the identity of the guerrillas chose death rather than betray their families and comrades. My father was such a man.

I was identified by an old school friend but managed to slip out to join others.

America's short-sighted businessmen were pleased with these developments, as they had the option to "redevelop" bombed-out areas—and insurance companies were absolved of their responsibilities for the ghetto property. The American labor movement supported the bombings because they eliminated the meager threat Black People have posed to the white American labor market. Most of the power brokers in the U.S. supported the actions of the government, for all gain and none lose as a result of innocent Black blood being shed.

Nevertheless, we continued to fight, attacking the production centers of America—sabotaging not only the American war effort in its own cities but American military operations around the world. Troops were diverted from foreign fronts and foreign bases to be concentrated in Negro ghetto areas.

World confidence in America's ability to contain its own domestic difficulties has ended and, with it, all confidence in the American dollar. An unprecedented assault upon the American economy has followed and, in a short time, the economy will fall. In the ruins of America, over the charred bodies of Americans, Black and white, over the trampled hopes and mangled dreams of an entire people, the few remaining will be charged with the responsibility of creating a new nation and a new world. . . .


There is no need for Americans, Black or white, to live through such hell. There is no reason to subject humanity to yet another holocaust. If Americans take advantage of trends already existing in this country, pending catastrophe can be converted to a national awakening.

In many counties of Mississippi and South Carolina, as well as other southern states, Black People are already in the majority. In these counties, rudimentary Black institutions already exist. If the electoral system in these areas is carefully safeguarded by the federal government, more Black Men will be elected to high office. There will be more Black sheriffs and more Black tax collectors. This development will no doubt result in large numbers of white people moving elsewhere—those whites who refuse to live and work with

Blacks. It should also result in the counter migration of urban Blacks to these areas in numbers at least sufficient to meet the manpower needs of the area. Within one generation there could well be two or three states that are Black led, Black controlled, and predominantly Black populated. Those whites who elected to stay would be welcome—they would be the whites willing to work together with Blacks for mutual progress.

During Reconstruction, Black Men wrote good laws and adopted them. They did not use their new-found power vindictively. It is likely that Black men today would also pass good laws, but this time, with Black Men in charge of their enforcement, the laws would also be enforced.

In these predominantly Black states, Blacks must own and control the large part of the economy. Political control without economic power is insufficient. The federal government could reimburse white southern businessmen who would relinquish their holdings to the Black Community. A Corporation Act could provide for the transfer of such property to Black shareholders and justly facilitate such transactions.

When Black People are in control of at least a few American states, they will be able to exert enough influence within the federal system to affect the treatment of their Black brothers in America's urban centers, as well as the exercise of American foreign policy. Of course, as we have said earlier, other radical changes will have to be made in order to facilitate such events.

It now remains to be seen if Americans will heed the warning. W. E. B. DuBois understood, in 1935, the only alternatives still available today.

Such mental frustration cannot indefinitely continue. Some day it may burst in fire and blood. Who will be to blame? And where the greater cost? Black folk, after all, have little to lose, but Civilization has all.

This the American black man knows; his fight here is a fight to the finish. Either he dies or wins. If he wins it will be by no subterfuge or evasion of amalgamation. He will enter modern civilization here in America as a black man on terms of perfect and unlimited equality with any white man, or he will enter not at all. Either extermination root and branch, or absolute equality. There can be no compromise. This is the last great battle of the West.

# Appendix

# The Declaration of Independence

When, in the course of human events, it becomes necessary for one people to dissolve the political bands which
have connected them with another, and to assume among
the powers of the earth, the separate and equal station to
which the laws of nature and of nature's God entitle them, a
decent respect to the opinions of mankind requires that they
should declare the causes which impel them to the separation.

We hold these truths to be self-evident, that all men are
created equal, that they are endowed by their Creator with
certain unalienable rights, that among these are life, liberty
and the pursuit of happiness. That to secure these rights,
governments are instituted among men, *deriving their just
powers from the consent of the governed, that whenever any
form of government becomes destructive of these ends, it is
the right of the people to alter or to abolish it, and to institute new government,* laying its foundation on such principles and organizing its powers in such form, as to them
shall seem most likely to effect their safety and happiness.
Prudence, indeed, will dictate that governments long established should not be changed for light and transient causes;
and accordingly all experience hath shown that mankind are
more disposed to suffer, while evils are sufferable, than to
right themselves by abolishing the forms to which they are
accustomed. *But when a long train of abuses and usurpations, pursuing invariably the same object evinces a design*

*to reduce them under absolute despotism,* it is their right, it is their duty, to throw off such government, and *to provide new guards for their future security.*—Such has been the patient sufferance of these colonies; and such is now the necessity which constrains them to alter their former systems of government. The history of the present King of Great Britain is a history of repeated injuries and usurpations, all having in direct object the establishment of an absolute tyranny over these states. To prove this, let facts be submitted to a candid world.

He has refused his assent to laws, the most wholesome and necessary for the public good.

He has forbidden his governors to pass laws of immediate and pressing importance, unless suspended in their operation till his assent should be obtained; and when so suspended, he has utterly neglected to attend to them.

He has refused to pass other laws for the accommodation of large districts of people, unless those people would relinquish the right of representation in the legislature, a right inestimable to them and formidable to tyrants only.

He has called together legislative bodies at places unusual, uncomfortable, and distant from the depository of their public records, for the sole purpose of fatiguing them into compliance with his measures.

He has dissolved representative houses repeatedly for opposing with manly firmness his invasions on the rights of the people.

He has refused for a long time, after such dissolutions, to cause others to be elected; whereby the legislative powers, incapable of annihilation, have returned to the people at large for their exercise; the state remaining in the meantime exposed to all the dangers of invasion from without, and convulsions within.

He has endeavored to prevent the population of these

states; for that purpose obstructing the laws for naturalization of foreigners; refusing to pass others to encourage their migration hither, and raising the conditions of new appropriations of lands.

He has obstructed the administration of justice, by refusing his assent to laws for establishing judiciary powers.

He has made judges dependent on his will alone, for the tenure of their offices, and the amount and payment of their salaries.

He has erected a multitude of new offices, and sent hither swarms of officers to harass our people, and eat out their substance.

He has kept among us, in times of peace, standing armies without the consent of our legislature.

He has affected to render the military independent of and superior to the civil power.

He has combined with others to subject us to a jurisdiction foreign to our constitution, and unacknowledged by our laws; giving his assent to their acts of pretended legislation:

For quartering large bodies of armed troops among us:

For protecting them, by a mock trial, from punishment for any murders which they should commit on the inhabitants of these states:

For cutting off our trade with all parts of the world:

For imposing taxes on us without our consent:

For depriving us in many cases, of the benefits of trial by jury:

For transporting us beyond seas to be tried for pretended offenses:

For abolishing the free system of English laws in a neighboring province, establishing therein an arbitrary government, and enlarging its boundaries so as to render it at once an example and fit instrument for introducing the same absolute rule into these colonies:

For taking away our charters, abolishing our most valuable laws, and altering fundamentally the forms of our governments:

For suspending our own legislatures, and declaring themselves invested with power to legislate for us in all cases whatsoever.

He has abdicated government here, by declaring us out of his protection and waging war against us.

He has plundered our seas, ravaged our coasts, burned our towns, and destroyed the lives of our people.

He is at this time transporting large armies of foreign mercenaries to complete the works of death, desolation and tyranny, already begun with circumstances of cruelty and perfidy scarcely paralleled in the most barbarous ages, and totally unworthy the head óf a civilized nation.

He has constrained our fellow citizens taken captive on the high seas to bear arms against their country, to become the executioners of their friends and brethren, or to fall themselves by their hands.

He has excited domestic insurrections amongst us, and has endeavored to bring on the inhabitants of our frontiers, the merciless Indian savages, whose known rule of warfare, is an undistinguished destruction of all ages, sexes and conditions.

In every stage of these oppressions we have petitioned for redress in the most humble terms: our repeated petitions have been answered only by repeated injury. A prince, whose character is thus marked by every act which may define a tryant, is unfit to be the ruler of a free people.

Nor have we been wanting in attention to our British brethren. We have warned them from time to time of attempts by their legislature to extend an unwarrantable jurisdiction over us. We have reminded them of the circumstances of our emigration and settlement here. We have appealed to their native justice and magnanimity, and we have conjured them by the ties of our common kindred to disavow these usurpations, which, would inevitably interrupt our connections and correspondence. They too have been deaf to the voice of justice and of consanguinity. We must, therefore, acquiesce in the necessity, which denounces our separation, and hold them, as we hold the rest of mankind, enemies in war, in peace friends.

We, therefore, the representatives of the United States of America, in General Congress, assembled, appealing to the Supreme Judge of the world for the rectitude of our intentions, do, in the name, and by the authority of the good people of these colonies, solemnly publish and declare, that these united colonies are, and of right ought to be free and independent states; that they are absolved from all allegiance to the British Crown, and that all political connection between them and the state of Great Britain, is and ought to be totally dissolved; and that as free and independent states, they have full power to levy war, conclude peace, contract alliances, establish commerce, and to do all other acts and things which independent states may of right do. And for the support of this declaration, with a firm reliance on the protection of Divine Providence, we mutually pledge to each other our lives, our fortunes and our sacred honor.

# The Constitution of the United States

WE THE PEOPLE of the United States, in order to form a more perfect Union, establish Justice, insure domestic Tranquility, provide for the common defence, promote the general Welfare, and secure the Blessing of Liberty to ourselves and our Posterity, do ordain and establish this Constitution for the United States of America.

## ARTICLE 1
## (THE LEGISLATURE)

### Section 1.

All legislative Powers herein granted shall be vested in a Congress of the United States, which shall consist of a Senate and House of Representatives.

### Section 2.

The House of Representatives shall be composed of Members chosen every second Year by the People of the several States, and the Electors in each State shall have the Qualifications requisite for Electors of the most numerous Branch of the State Legislature.

No Person shall be a Representative who shall not have attained to the Age of twenty-five Years, and been seven Years a Citizen of the United States, and who shall not, when elected, be an Inhabitant of that State in which he shall be chosen.

[Representatives and direct Taxes shall be apportioned among the several States which may be included within this Union, according to their respective Numbers, which shall be determined by adding to the whole Number of free Persons, including those bound to Service for a Term of Years, and excluding Indians not taxed, three fifths of all other persons.][1] The actual Enumeration shall be made within three Years after the first Meeting of the Congress of the United States, and within every subsequent Term of ten Years, in such Manner as they shall by Law direct. The Number of Representatives shall not exceed one for every thirty thousand, but each State shall have at Least one Representative; and until such enumeration shall be made, the State of New Hampshire shall be entitled to chuse three, Massachusetts eight, Rhode Island and Providence Plantations one, Connecticut five, New York six, New Jersey four, Pennsylvania eight, Delaware one, Maryland six, Virginia ten, North Carolina five, South Carolina five, and Georgia three.

When vacancies happen in the Representation from any State, the Executive Authority thereof shall issue Writs of Election to fill such Vacancies.

The House of Representatives shall chuse their Speaker and other Officers; and shall have the sole Power of Impeachment.

## Section 3.

The Senate of the United States shall be composed of two Senators from each State, chosen by the Legislature thereof,[2] for six Years; and each Senator shall have one Vote.

---

[1] Altered by Amendment XVI. The three-fifths rule was eliminated by Amendments XIII and XIV.
[2] See Amendment XVII.

Immediately after they shall be assembled in Consequence of the first Election, they shall be divided as equally as may be into three Classes. The Seats of the Senators of the first Class shall be vacated at the Expiration of the second Year, of the Second Class at the Expiration of the fourth Year, and of the third Class at the Expiration of the sixth Year, so that one-third may be chosen every second Year; and if Vacancies happen by Resignation, or otherwise, during the Recess of the Legislature of any State, the Executive thereof may make temporary Appointments until the next Meeting of the Legislature, which shall then fill such Vacancies.

No Person shall be a Senator who shall not have attained to the Age of thirty Years, and been nine Years a Citizen of the United States, and who shall not, when elected, be an Inhabitant of that State for which he shall be chosen.

The Vice-President of the United States shall be President of the Senate, but shall have no Vote, unless they be equally divided.

The Senate shall chuse their other Officers, and also a President pro tempore, in the absence of the Vice-President, or when he shall exercise the Office of President of the United States.

The Senate shall have the sole Power to try all Impeachments. When sitting for that Purpose, they shall be on Oath or Affirmation. When the President of the United States is tried, the Chief Justice shall preside; And no Person shall be convicted without the Concurrence of two thirds of the Members present.

Judgment in Cases of Impeachment shall not extend further than to removal from Office, and disqualification to hold and enjoy any Office of honor, Trust or Profit under the United States: but the Party convicted shall nevertheless be liable and subject to Indictment, Trial, Judgment and Punishment, according to Law.

## Section 4.

The Times, Places and Manner of holding Elections for Senators and Representatives, shall be prescribed in each State by the Legislature thereof; but the Congress may at any time by Law make or alter such Regulations, except as to the Places of Chusing Senators.

The Congress shall assemble at least once in every Year, and such Meeting shall be on the first Monday in December, unless they shall by Law appoint a different Day.[3]

## Section 5.

Each House shall be the Judge of the Elections, Returns and Qualifications of its own Members, and a Majority of each shall constitute a Quorum to do Business; but a smaller Number may adjourn from day to day, and may be authorized to compel the Attendance of absent Members, in such Manner, and under such Penalties as each House may provide.

Each House may determine the Rules of its Proceedings, punish its Members for disorderly Behavior, and, with the Concurrence of two thirds, expel a Member.

Each House shall keep a Journal of its Proceedings and from time to time publish the same, excepting such Parts as may in their Judgment require Secrecy; and the Yeas and Nays of the Members of either House on any question shall, at the Desire of one fifth of those Present, be entered on the journal.

Neither House, during the Session of Congress, shall without the Consent of the other, adjourn for more than three

[3] See Amendment XX.

days, nor to any other Place than that in which the two Houses shall be sitting.

## Section 6.

The Senators and Representatives shall receive a Compensation for their Services, to be ascertained by Law, and paid out of the Treasury of the United States. They shall in all Cases, except Treason, Felony, and Breach of the peace, be privileged from Arrest during their Attendance at the Session of their respective Houses, and in going to and returning from the same; and for any Speech or Debate in either House, they shall not be questioned in any other Place.

No Senator or Representative shall, during the Time for which he was elected, be appointed to any civil Office under the Authority of the United States, which shall have been created, or the Emoluments whereof shall have been encreased during such time; and no Person holding any Office under the United States, shall be a Member of either House during his Continuance in Office.

## Section 7.

All Bills for raising Revenue shall originate in the House of Representatives; but the Senate may propose or concur with Amendments as on other Bills.

Every Bill which shall have passed the House of Representatives and the Senate, shall, before it become a Law, be presented to the President of the United States; If he approve he shall sign it, but if not he shall return it, with his Objections to that House in which it shall have originated, who shall enter the Objections at large on their Journal, and proceed to reconsider it. If after such Reconsideration two thirds of that House shall agree to pass the Bill it shall be sent, together with the Objections, to the other House, by which it shall likewise be reconsidered, and if approved by two-thirds of that House, it shall become a Law. But in all such Cases the Votes of both Houses shall be determined by Yeas and Nays, and the Names of the Persons voting for and against the Bill shall be entered on the Journal of each House respectively. If any Bill shall not be returned by the President within ten Days (Sundays excepted) after it shall have been presented to him, the Same shall be a Law, in like Manner as if he had signed it, unless the Congress by their Adjournment prevent its Return, in which Case it shall not be a Law.

Every Order, Resolution, or Vote to which the Concurrence of the Senate and House of Representatives may be necessary (except on a question of Adjournment) shall be presented to the President of the United States: and before the Same shall take Effect shall be approved by him, or being disapproved by him, shall be repassed by two thirds of the Senate and House of Representatives, according to the Rules and Limitations prescribed in the Case of a Bill.

### Section 8.

The Congress shall have Power To lay and collect Taxes, Duties, Imposts and Excises, to pay the Debts and provide for the common Defence and general Welfare of the United States; but all Duties, Imposts and Excises shall be uniform throughout the United States;

To borrow money on the Credit of the United States;

To regulate Commerce with foreign Nations, and among the several States, and with the Indian Tribes;

To establish an uniform Rule of Naturalization, and uniform Laws on the subject of Bankruptcies throughout the United States;

To coin Money, regulate the Value thereof, and of foreign Coin, and fix the Standard of Weights and Measures;

To provide for the Punishment of counterfeiting the Securities and current Coin of the United States;

To establish Post Officers and post Roads;

To promote the Progress of Science and useful arts, by securing for limited Times to Authors and Inventors the exclusive Right to their respective Writings and Discoveries;

To constitute Tribunals inferior to the supreme Court;

To define and punish Piracies and Felonies committed on the high Seas, and Offenses against the Law of Nations;

To declare War, grant Letters of Marque and Reprisal, and make Rules concerning Captures on Land and Water;

To raise and support Armies, but no Appropriation of Money to that Use shall be for a longer Term than two Years;

To provide and maintain a Navy;

To make Rules for the Government and Regulation of the land and naval Forces;

To provide for calling forth the Militia to execute the Laws of the Union, suppress Insurrections and repel Invasions;

To provide for organizing, arming, and disciplining the Militia, and for governing such Part of them as may be employed in the Service of the United States, reserving to the States respectively, the Appointment of the Officers, and the Authority of training the Militia according to the discipline prescribed by Congress;

To exercise exclusive Legislation in all Cases whatsoever, over such District (not exceeding ten Miles square) as may, by Cession of particular States, and the acceptance of Congress, become the Seat of the Government of the United States, and to exercise like Authority over all Places purchased by the Consent of the Legislature of the State in which the Same shall be, for the Erection of Forts, Magazines, Arsenals, dock-Yards, and other needful Buildings; —And

To make all Laws which shall be necessary and proper for carrying into Execution the foregoing Powers, and all other Powers vested by this Constitution in the Government of the United States, or in any Department or Officer thereof.

## Section 9.

The Migration or Importation of such Persons as any of the States now existing shall think proper to admit, shall not be prohibited by the Congress prior to the Year one thousand eight hundred and eight, but a tax or duty may be imposed on such Importation, not exceeding ten dollars for each Person.

The privilege of the Writ of Habeas Corpus shall not be suspended, unless when in Cases of Rebellion or Invasion the public Safety may require it.

No Bill of Attainder or ex post facto Law shall be passed.

No capitation, or other direct Tax shall be laid, unless in Proportion to the Census or Enumeration herein before directed to be taken.[4]

No Tax or Duty shall be laid on Articles exported from any State.

No Preference shall be given by any Regulation of Commerce or Revenue to the Ports of one State over those of another: nor shall Vessels bound to, or from one State, be obliged to enter, clear, or pay Duties in another.

No Money shall be drawn from the Treasury, but in Consequence of Appropriations made by Law; and a regular Statement and Account of the Receipts and Expenditures of all public Money shall be published from time to time.

No Title of Nobility shall be granted by the United States: And no Person holding any Office of Profit or Trust under them, shall, without the consent of the Congress, accept of

---

[4] See Amendment XVI.

any present, Emolument, Office, or Title, of any kind whatever, from any King, Prince, or foreign State.

## Section 10.

No State shall enter into any Treaty, Alliance, or Confederation; grant Letters of Marque and Reprisal; coin Money; emit Bills of Credit; make any Thing but gold and silver Coin a Tender in Payment of Debts; pass any Bill of Attainder, ex post facto Law, or Law impairing the Obligation of Contracts, or grant any Title of Nobility.

No State shall, without the Consent of the Congress, lay any Imposts or Duties on Imports or Exports, except what may be absolutely necessary for executing its inspection Laws: and the net Produce of all Duties and Imposts, laid by any State on Imports or Exports, shall be for the Use of the Treasury of the United States and all such Laws shall be subject to the Revision and Controul of the Congress.

No State shall, without the Consent of Congress, lay any duty of Tonnage, keep Troops, or Ships of War in time of Peace, enter into any Agreement or Compact with another State, or with a foreign Power, or engage in War, unless actually invaded, or in such imminent Danger as will not admit of delay.

## ARTICLE 2
### (THE EXECUTIVE)

## Section 1.

The executive Power shall be vested in a President of the United States of America. He shall hold his Office during the Term of four Years, and, together with the Vice-President, chosen for the same Term, be elected, as follows

Each State shall appoint, in such Manner as the Legislature thereof may direct, a Number of Electors, equal to the whole number of Senators and Representatives to which the State may be entitled in the Congress; but no Senator or Representative, or Person holding an Office of Trust or Profit under the United States, shall be appointed an Elector.

[The Electors shall meet in their respective States, and vote by Ballot for two persons, of whom one at least shall not be an Inhabitant of the same State with themselves. And they shall make a List of all the Persons voted for, and of the Number of Votes for each; which List they shall sign and certify, and transmit sealed to the Seat of the Government of the United States, directed to the President of the Senate. The President of the Senate shall, in the Presence of the Senate and House of Representatives, open all the Certificates, and the Votes shall then be counted. The person having the greatest number of Votes shall be the President, if such Number be a Majority of the whole Number of Electors appointed; and if there be more than one who have such Majority, and have an Equal Number of Votes, then the House of Representatives shall immediately chuse by Ballot one of them for President; and if no Person have a Majority, then from the five highest on the List the said House shall in like Manner chuse the President, but in chusing the President, the Votes shall be taken by States, the Representation from each State having one Vote; A quorum for this Purpose shall consist of a Member or Members from two-thirds of the States, and a Majority of all the States shall be necessary to a Choice. In every Case, after the Choice of the President, the Person having the greatest number of Votes of the Electors shall be the Vice-President. But if there should remain two or more who have equal Votes, the Senate shall chuse from them by Ballot the Vice-President.][5]

The Congress may determine the Time of chusing the

[5] Superseded by Amendment XII.

Electors, and the Day on which they shall give their Vote; which Day shall be the same throughout the United States.

No person except a natural born Citizen, or a Citizen of the United States, at the time of the Adoption of this Constitution, shall be eligible to the Office of President; neither shall any Person be eligible to that Office who shall not have attained to the Age of thirty-five Years, and been fourteen Years a Resident within the United States.

In Case of the Removal of the President from Office, or of his Death, Resignation, or Inability to discharge the Powers and Duties of the said office, the same shall devolve on the Vice-President, and the Congress may by Law provide for the Case of Removal, Death, Resignation or Inability, both of the President and Vice-President, declaring what Officer shall then act as President, and such Officer shall act accordingly until the Disability be removed, or a President shall be elected.

The President shall, at stated Times, receive for his Services, a Compensation, which shall neither be encreased nor diminished during the Period for which he shall have been elected, and he shall not receive with that Period any other Emolument from the United States, or any of them.

Before he enter on the Execution of his Office, he shall take the following Oath or Affirmation:—"I do solemnly swear (or affirm) that I will faithfully execute the Office of President of the United States, and will to the best of my Ability, preserve, protect and defend the Constitution of the United States."

*Section 2.*

The President shall be Commander in Chief of the Army and Navy of the United States, and of the Militia of the several states, when called into the actual Service of the

United States; he may require the Opinion in writing, of the principal Officer in each of the executive Departments, upon any subject relating to the Duties of their respective Offices, and he shall have Power to Grant Reprieves and Pardons for Offenses against the United States, except in Cases of Impeachment.

He shall have Power, by and with the advice and Consent of the Senate, to make Treaties, provided two-thirds of the Senators present concur; and he shall nominate, and by and with the Advice and Consent of the Senate, shall appoint Ambassadors, other public Ministers and Consuls, Judges of the supreme Court and all other Officers of the United States, whose Appointments are not herein otherwise provided for, and which shall be established by Law: but the Congress may by Law vest the Appointment of such inferior Officers, as they think proper, in the President alone, in the Courts of Law, or in the Heads of Departments.

The President shall have Power to fill up all Vacancies that may happen during the Recess of the Senate by granting Commissions which shall expire at the End of their next Session.

## Section 3.

He shall from time to time give to the Congress Information of the State of the Union, and recommend to their Consideration such Measures as he shall judge necessary and expedient; he may, on extraordinary Occasions, convene both Houses, or either of them, and in Cases of Disagreement between them, with Respect to the Time of Adjournment, he may adjourn them to such Time as he shall think proper; he shall receive Ambassadors and other public Ministers; he shall take Care that the Laws be faithfully executed, and shall Commission all the Officers of the United States.

## Section 4.

The President, Vice-President and all civil Officers of the United States, shall be removed from Office on Impeachment for, and Conviction of, Treason, Bribery, or other high Crimes and Misdemeanors.

## ARTICLE 3
### (THE JUDICIARY)

### Section 1.

The judicial Power of the United States shall be vested in one supreme Court, and in such inferior Courts as the Congress may from time to time ordain and establish. The Judges, both of the supreme and inferior Courts, shall hold their offices during good Behaviour, and shall, at stated Times, receive for the Services a Compensation which shall not be diminished during their Continuance in Office.

### Section 2.

The judicial Power shall extend to all Cases, in Law and Equity, arising under this Constitution, the Law of the United States and Treaties made, or which shall be made, under their Authority;—to all Cases affecting Ambassadors, other public Ministers and Consuls—to all Cases of admirality and maritime Jurisdiction—to Controversies to which the United States shall be a Party;—to Controversies between two or more States;—between a State and Citizens of another state;[6]—Between Citizens of different States;—

---

[6] See Amendment XI.

between Citizens of the same State claiming Lands under Grants of different States, and between a State, or the Citizens thereof, and foreign States, Citizens or Subjects.

In all Cases affecting Ambassadors, other public Ministers and Consuls, and those in which a State shall be Party, the supreme Court shall have original Jurisdiction. In all the other Cases before mentioned, the supreme Court shall have appellate Jurisdiction, both as to Law and Fact, with such Exceptions, and under such Regulations as the Congress shall make.

The trial of all Crimes, except in Cases of Impeachment, shall be by Jury, and such Trial shall be held in the State where the said Crimes shall have been committed; but when not committed within any State, the Trial shall be at such Place or Places as the Congress may by Law have directed.

## Section 3.

Treason against the United States, shall consist only in levying War against them, or in adhering to their Enemies, giving them Aid and Comfort. No Person shall be convicted of Treason unless on the Testimony of two Witnesses to the same overt Act, or on Confession in open Court.

The Congress shall have power to declare the Punishment of Treason, but no Attainder of Treason shall work Corruption of Blood, or Forfeiture except during the Life of the Person attainted.

## ARTICLE 4
### (THE STATES)

## Section 1.

Full Faith and Credit shall be given in each State to the public acts, Records, and judicial Proceedings of every other State. And the Congress may by general Laws prescribe the Manner in which such Acts, Records and Proceedings shall be proved, and the Effect thereof.

## Section 2.

The Citizens of each State shall be entitled to all Privileges and Immunities of Citizens in the several States.

A Person charged in any State with Treason, Felony, or other Crime, who shall flee from Justice, and be found in another State, shall on demand of the executive Authority of the State from which he fled, be delivered up, to be removed to the State having Jurisdiction of the Crime.

No Person held to Service or Labour in one State, under the Laws thereof, escaping into another, shall, in Consequence of any Law or Regulation therein, be discharged from such Service or Labour, but shall be delivered up on Claim of the Party to whom such Service or Labour may be due.[7]

## Section 3.

New States may be admitted by the Congress into this Union; but no new States shall be formed or erected within the Jurisdiction of any other State; nor any State be formed by the Junction of two or more States, or parts of States, without the Consent of the Legislatures of the States concerned as well as of the Congress.

The Congress shall have Power to dispose of and make all needful Rules and Regulations respecting the Territory or other Property belonging to the United States; and nothing in this Constitution shall be so constructed as to Prejudice any Claims of the United States, or of particular State.

[7] Superseded by Amendment XIII.

## Section 4.

The United States shall guarantee to every State in this Union a Republican Form of Government, and shall protect each of them against Invasion; and on Application of the Legislature, or of the Executive (when the Legislature cannot be convened) against domestic Violence.

### ARTICLE 5
### (AMENDMENTS)

The Congress whenever two-thirds of both Houses shall deem it necessary, shall propose Amendments to this Constitution, or, on the Application of the Legislatures of two-thirds of the several States, shall call a Convention for proposing Amendments, which, in either Case, shall be valid to all Intents and Purposes, as part of this Constitution, when ratified by the Legislatures of three-fourths of the several States, or by Conventions in three-fourths thereof, as the one or the other Mode of Ratification may be proposed by the Congress; Provided that no Amendment which may be made prior to the Year One thousand eight hundred and eight shall in any Manner affect the first and fourth Clauses in the Ninth Section of the first Article; and that no State, without its Consent, shall be deprived of its equal Suffrage in the Senate.

### ARTICLE 6
### (PUBLIC DEBT, THE SUPREMACY CLAUSE,
### OATHS, RELIGIOUS TESTS)

All Debts contracted and Engagements entered into, before the Adoption of this Constitution, shall be as valid against the United States under this Constitution, as under the Confederation.

*This Constitution, and the Laws of the United States which shall be made in Pursuance thereof; and all Treaties made, or which shall be made, under the Authority of the United States, shall be the supreme Law of the Land; and the Judges in every State shall be bound thereby, any Thing in the Constitution or Laws of any State to the Contrary notwithstanding.*

The Senators and Representatives before mentioned, and the Members of the several State Legislatures, and all executive and judicial Officers, both of the United States and of the several States, shall be bound by Oath or Affirmation, to support this Constitution; but no religious Test shall ever be required as a Qualification to any Office or public Trust under the United States.

### ARTICLE 7
### (RATIFICATION)

The Ratification of the Conventions of nine States shall be sufficient for the Establishment of this Constitution between the states so ratifying the Same.

Done in Convention by the Unanimous Consent of the States present the Seventeenth Day of September in the Year of our Lord one thousand seven hundred and Eighty seven and of the Independence of the United States of America the Twelfth. In Witness whereof We have hereunto subscribed our Names [omitted here].

### AMENDMENT I[8]

Congress shall make no law respecting an establishment of religion, or prohibiting the free exercise thereof; or abridging the freedom of speech, or of the press; or the right of the

---

[8] The first ten Amendments were adopted in 1791.

people peaceably to assemble, and to petition the Government for a redress of grievances.

## AMENDMENT II

A well regulated Militia, being necessary to the security of a free State, the right of the people to keep and bear Arms, shall not be infringed.

## AMENDMENT III

No Soldier shall, in time of peace be quartered in any house, without the consent of the Owner, nor in time of war, but in a manner to be prescribed by law.

## AMENDMENT IV

The right of the people to be secure in their persons, houses, papers, and effects, against unreasonable searches and seizures, shall not be violated, and no Warrants shall issue, but upon probable cause, supported by Oath or affirmation, and particularly describing the place to be searched, and the persons or things to be seized.

## AMENDMENT V

No person shall be held to answer for a capital, or otherwise infamous crime, unless on a presentment or indictment of a Grand Jury, except in cases arising in the land or naval forces, or in the Militia, when in actual service in time of war or public danger; nor shall any person be subject for the same offense to be twice put in jeopardy of life or limb, nor shall be compelled in any criminal case to be a witness against himself, nor be deprived of life, liberty, or property, without the due process of law; nor shall private property be taken for public use, without just compensation.

## AMENDMENT VI

In all criminal prosecutions, the accused shall enjoy the right to a speedy and public trial, by an imparital jury of the State and district wherein the crime shall have been committed, which district shall have been previously ascertained by law, and to be informed of the nature and cause of the accusation; to be confronted with the witnesses against him; to have the compulsory process for obtaining witnesses in his favor, and to have the Assistance of Counsel for his defence.

## AMENDMENT VII

In suits at common law, where the value in controversy shall exceed twenty dollars, the right of trial by jury shall be preserved, and no fact tried by a jury, shall be otherwise reexamined in Any Court of the United States, than according to the rules of the common law.

## AMENDMENT VIII

Excessive bail shall not be required, nor excessive fines imposed, nor cruel and unusual punishments inflicted.

## AMENDMENT IX

The enumeration in the Constitution, of certain rights shall not be construed to deny or disparage others retained by the people.

## AMENDMENT X

The powers not delegated to the United States by the Constitution, nor prohibited by it to the States, are reserved to the States respectively, or to the people.

## AMENDMENT XI[9]

The Judicial power of the United States shall not be construed to extend to any suit in law or equity, commenced or prosecuted against one of the United States by Citizens of another State, or by Citizens or Subjects of any Foreign States.

## AMENDMENT XII[10]

The Electors shall meet in their respective states and vote by ballot for President and Vice-President, one of whom, at least, shall not be an inhabitant of the same state with themselves; they shall name in their ballots the person voted for as President and in distinct ballots the person voted for as Vice-President, and they shall make distinct lists of all persons voted for as President, and of all persons voted for as Vice-President, and of the number of votes for each, which lists they shall sign and certify, and transmit sealed to the seat of the government of the United States, directed to the President of the Senate;—The President of the Senate shall, in the presence of the Senate and House of Representatives, open all the certificates and the votes shall then be counted;—The person having the greatest number of votes for President, shall be the President, if such number be a majority of the

[9] Adopted 1798.
[10] Adopted 1804.

whole number of Electors appointed; and if no person have such majority, then from the persons having the highest numbers not exceeding three on the list of those voted for as President, the House of Representatives shall choose immediately, by ballot, the President. But in choosing the President, the votes shall be taken by states, the representation from each state having one vote; a quorum for this purpose shall consist of a member or members from two-thirds of the states, and a majority of all the states shall be necessary to a choice. And if the House of Representatives shall not choose a President whenever the right of choice shall devolve upon them, before the fourth day of March next following, then the Vice-President shall act as President, as in the case of the death or other constitutional disability of the President.—The person having the greatest number of votes as Vice-President, shall be the Vice-President, if such number be a majority of the whole number of Electors appointed, and if no person have a majority, then from the two highest numbers on the list, the Senate shall choose the Vice-President; a quorum for the purpose shall consist of two-thirds of the whole number of Senators, and a majority of the whole number shall be necessary to a choice. But no person constitutionally ineligible to the office of President shall be eligible to that of Vice-President of the United States.

## AMENDMENT XIII[11]

### Section 1.

Neither slavery nor involuntary servitude, except as a punishment for crime whereof the party shall have been duly convicted, shall exist within the United States, or any place subject to their jurisdiction.

[11] Adopted 1865.

## Section 2.

Congress shall have power to enforce this article by appropriate legislation.

## AMENDMENT XIV[12]

## Section 1.

All persons born or naturalized in the United States and subject to the jurisdiction thereof, are citizens of the United States and of the State wherein they reside. No State shall make or enforce any law which shall abridge the privileges or immunities of citizens of the United States; nor shall any State deprive any person of life, liberty or property, without the due process of law; nor deny to any person within its jurisdiction the equal protection of the laws.

## Section 2.

Representatives shall be apportioned among the several States according to their respective numbers, counting the whole number of persons in each State, excluding Indians not taxed. But when the right to vote at any election for the choice of electors for President and Vice-President of the United States, Representatives in Congress, the Executive and Judicial Officers of a State, or the members of the Legislature thereof, is denied to any of the male inhabitants of such State, being twenty-one years of age, and citizens of the United States, or in any way abridged, except for participation in rebellion, or other crime, the basis of representation therein shall be reduced in the proportion which the

---

[12] Adopted 1868.

number of such male citizens shall bear to the whole number of male citizens twenty-one years of age in such State.

## Section 3.

No person shall be a Senator or Representative in Congress, or elector of President and Vice-President, or hold any office, civil or military, under the United States, or under any State, who, having previously taken an oath, as a member of Congress, or as an officer of the United States, or as a member of any State legislature, or as an executive or judicial officer of any State, to support the Constitution of the United States, shall have engaged in insurrection or rebellion against the same, or given aid or comfort to the enemies thereof. But Congress may by a vote of two-thirds of each House, remove such disability.

## Section 4.

The validity of the public debt of the United States, authorized by law, including debts incurred for payment of pensions and bounties for services in suppressing insurrection or rebellion, shall not be questioned. But neither the United States nor any State shall assume or pay any debt or obligation incurred in aid of insurrection or rebellion against the United States, or any claim for the loss or emancipation of any slave; but all such debts, obligations and claims shall be held illegal and void.

## Section 5.

The Congress shall have power to enforce, by appropriate legislation, the provisions of this article.

## AMENDMENT XV[13]

### Section 1.

The right of citizens of the United States to vote shall not be denied or abridged by the United States or by any State on account of race, color, or previous condition of servitude.

### Section 2.

The Congress shall have power to enforce this article by appropriate legislation.

## AMENDMENT XVI[14]

The Congress shall have power to lay and collect taxes on incomes, from whatever source derived, without apportionment among the several States, and without regard to any census or enumeration.

## AMENDMENT XVII[15]

The Senate of the United States shall be composed of two Senators from each State, elected by the people thereof, for six years, and each Senator shall have one vote. The electors in each State shall have the qualifications requisite for electors of the most numerous branch of the State legislatures.

When vacancies happen in the representation of any State in the Senate, the executive authority of such State shall issue writs of election to fill such vacancies: Provided, That the legislature of any State may empower the executive

[13] Adopted 1870.
[14] Adopted 1913.
[15] Adopted 1913.

thereof to make temporary appointments until the people fill the vacancies by election as the legislature may direct.

This amendment shall not be so construed as to affect the election or term of any Senator chosen before it becomes valid as part of the Constitution.

## AMENDMENT XVIII[16]

### Section 1.

After one year from the ratification of this article the manufacture, sale, or transportation of intoxicating liquors within, the importation thereof into, or the exportation thereof from the United States and all territory subject to the jurisdiction thereof for beverage purposes is hereby prohibited.

### Section 2.

The Congress and the several States shall have concurrent power to enforce this article by appropriate legislation.

### Section 3.

This article shall be inoperative unless it shall have been ratified as an amendment to the Constitution by the legislatures of the several States, as provided in the Constitution, within seven years from the date of the submission hereof to the States by the Congress.

[16] Adopted in 1919. Repealed by the Twenty-first Amendment.

## AMENDMENT XIX[17]

The right of citizens of the United States to vote shall not be denied or abridged by the United States or by any State on account of sex.

Congress shall have power to enforce this article by appropriate legislation.

## AMENDMENT XX[18]

### Section 1.

The terms of the President and Vice-President shall end at noon on the 20th of January, and the terms of Senators and Representatives at noon on the 3d day of January, of the years in which such terms would have ended if this article had not been ratified; and the terms of their successors shall then begin.

### Section 2.

The Congress shall assemble at least once in every year, and such meeting shall begin at noon on the 3d day of January, unless they shall by law appoint a different day.

### Section 3.

If, at the time fixed for the beginning of the term of the President, the President elect shall have died, the Vice-President elect shall become President. If a President shall not have been chosen before the time fixed for the beginning of his term, or if the President elect shall have failed to qualify, then the Vice-President elect shall act as President until a President shall have qualified; and the Congress may

[17] Adopted 1920.
[18] Adopted 1933.

by law provide for the case wherein neither a President elect nor a Vice-President elect shall have qualified, declaring who shall then act as President, or the manner in which one who is to act shall be selected, and such person shall act accordingly until a President or Vice-President shall have qualified.

## Section 4.

The Congress may by law provide for the case of the death of any of the persons from whom the House of Representatives may choose a President whenever the right of choice shall have devolved upon them, and for the case of the death of any of the persons from whom the Senate may choose a Vice-President whenever the right of choice shall have devolved upon them.

## Section 5.

Sections 1 and 2 shall take effect on the 15th day of October following the ratification of this article.

## Section 6.

This article shall be inoperative unless it shall have been ratified as an amendment to the Constitution by the legislatures of three-fourths of the several States within seven years from the date of its submission.

## AMENDMENT XXI[19]

## Section 1.

The eighteenth article of amendment to the Constitution of the United States is hereby repealed.

[19] Adopted 1933.

## Section 2.

The transportation or importation into any State, Territory, or possession of the United States for delivery or use therein of intoxicating liquors, in violation of the laws thereof, is hereby prohibited.

## Section 3.

This article shall be inoperative unless it shall have been ratified as an amendment to the Constitution by conventions in the several States, as provided in the Constitution, within seven years from the date of the submission hereof to the States by the Congress.

## AMENDMENT XXII[20]

## Section 1.

No person shall be elected to the office of the President more than twice, and no person who has held the office of President, or acted as President, for more than two years of a term to which some other person was elected President shall be elected to the office of the President more than once. But this Article shall not apply to any person holding the office of President when this Article was proposed by the Congress, and shall not prevent any person who may be holding the Office of President, or acting as President, during the term within which this Article becomes operative from holding the office of President, or acting as President during the remainder of such term.

[20] Adopted 1951.

## Section 2.

This Article shall be inoperative unless it shall have been ratified as an amendment to the Constitution by the legislatures of three-fourths of the several States within seven years from the date of its submission to the States by the Congress.

## AMENDMENT XXIII[21]

## Section 1.

The District constituting the seat of Government of the United States shall appoint in such manner as the Congress may direct:

A number of electors of President and Vice President equal to the whole number of Senators and Representatives in Congress to which the District would be entitled if it were a State, but in no event more than the least populous State; they shall be in addition to those appointed by the States, but they shall be considered, for the purposes of the election of President and Vice President, to be electors appointed by a State; and they shall meet in the District and perform such duties as provided by the twelfth article of amendment.

## Section 2.

The Congress shall have power to enforce this article by appropriate legislation.

[21] Adopted 1961.

## AMENDMENT XXIV[22]

### Section 1.

The right of citizens of the United States to vote in any primary or other election for President or Vice President, for electors for President or Vice President, or for Senator or Representative in Congress, shall not be denied or abridged by the United States or any state by reason of failure to pay any poll tax or other tax.

### Section 2.

The Congress shall have power to enforce this article by appropriate legislation.

[22] Adopted 1964.

# Emancipation Proclamation

## BY THE PRESIDENT OF THE UNITED STATES OF AMERICA:

### A PROCLAMATION.

Whereas on the 22d day of September, A.D. 1862, a proclamation was issued by the President of the United States, containing, among other things, the following, to wit:

"That on the 1st day of January, A.D. 1863, all persons held as slaves within any State or designated part of a State the people whereof shall then be in rebellion against the United States shall be then, thenceforward, and forever free; and the executive government of the United States, including the military and naval authority thereof, will recognize and maintain the freedom of such persons and will do no acts to repress such persons, or any of them, in any efforts they may make for their actual freedom.

"That the executive will on the 1st day of January aforesaid, by proclamation, designate the States and parts of the States, if any, in which the people thereof, respectively, shall then be in rebellion against the United States; and the fact that any State or the people thereof shall on that day be in good faith represented in the Congress of the United States by members chosen thereto at elections wherein a majority of the qualified voters of such States shall have participated shall, in the absence of strong countervailing testimony, be deemed conclusive evidence that such State and the people thereof are not then in rebellion against the United States."

Now, therefore, I, Abraham Lincoln, President of the United States, by virtue of the power in me vested as Commander-in-Chief of the Army and Navy of the United States in time of actual armed rebellion against authority and government of the United States, and as a fit and necessary war measure for suppressing said rebellion, do, on this 1st day of January, A.D. 1863, and in accordance with my purpose so to do, publicly proclaimed for the full period of one hundred days from the first day above mentioned, order and designate as the States and parts of States wherein the people thereof, respectively, are this day in rebellion against the United States the following, to wit:

Arkansas, Texas, Louisiana (except the parishes of St. Bernard, Plaquemines, Jefferson, St. John, St. Charles, St. James, Ascension, Assumption, Terrebonne, Lafourche, St. Mary, St. Martin, and Orleans, including the city of New Orleans), Mississippi, Alabama, Florida, Georgia, South Carolina, North Carolina, and Virginia (except the forty-eight counties designated as West Virginia, and also the counties of Berkeley, Accomac, Northhampton, Elizabeth City, York, Princess Anne, and Norfolk, including the cities of Norfolk and Portsmouth), and which excepted parts are for the present left precisely as if this proclamation were not issued.

And by virtue of the power and for the purpose aforesaid, I do order and declare that all persons held as slaves within said designated States and parts of States are, and henceforward shall be, free; and that the Executive Government of the United States, including the military and naval authorities thereof, will recognize and maintain the freedom of said persons.

And I hereby enjoin upon the people so declared to be free to abstain from all violence, unless in necessary self-defense; and I recommend to them that, in all cases when allowed, they labor faithfully for reasonable wages.

And I further declare and make known that such persons

of suitable condition will be received into the armed service of the United States to garrison forts, positions, stations, and other places, and to man vessels of all sorts in said service.

And upon this act, sincerely believed to be an act of justice, warranted by the Constitution upon military necessity, I invoke the considerate judgment of mankind and the gracious favor of Almighty God.

# Bibliography

Aptheker, Herbert. *American Negro Slave Revolts.* New York, Columbia University Press, 1943.

———. *A Documentary History of the Negro in the United States.* New York, Citadel Press, 1951.

———. *To Be Free.* New York, International Publishers, 1948.

Baldwin, James. *The Fire Next Time.* New York, Dial Press, 1963.

———. *Notes of a Native Son.* Boston, Beacon Press, 1955.

Bell, Howard H. "Negro Nationalism: A Factor in Emigration Projects, 1858–1861," *Journal of Negro History,* XLVII (January, 1962), 42–53.

Bennett, Lerone, Jr. *Before the Mayflower.* Chicago, Johnson Publishing Company, 1964.

———. *Confrontation Black and White.* Chicago, Johnson Publishing Company, 1965.

Beth, Loren P. *Politics and the Supreme Court.* New York, Harper & Row, 1962.

Breitman, George, ed. *Malcolm X Speaks.* New York, Grove Press, 1966.

Broderick, Francis L., and August Meier. *Negro Protest Thought in the Twentieth Century.* New York, Bobbs-Merrill, 1965.

———. *W. E. B. DuBois, Negro Leader.* Stanford, Calif., Stanford University Press, 1966.

Clark, Kenneth B. *Dark Ghetto: Dilemmas of Social Power.* New York, Harper & Row, 1965.

Conrad, Earl. *The Invention of the Negro.* New York, Paul S. Eriksson, 1966.

Cronon, Edmund David. *Black Moses.* Madison, University of Wisconsin Press, 1966.

*Cushman's Leading Constitutional Decisions.* 13th ed. New York, Meredith Publishing Company, 1966.

Danzig, David. "In Defense of 'Black Power,'" *Commentary*, 42 (September, 1966), 41–46.

Douglass, Frederick. *Life and Times of Frederick Douglass, Written by Himself.* Boston, De Wolfe & Co., 1895.

Drake, St. Clair, and Horace Cayton. *Black Metropolis: A Study of Negro Life in a Northern City.* Vol. I (revised and enlarged edition). New York, Harper Torchbooks, 1962.

DuBois, W. E. B. *The Autobiography of W. E. B. DuBois.* New York, International Publishers, 1965.

———. *Black Folk: Then and Now.* New York, Henry Holt, 1939.

———. *Black Reconstruction in America 1860–1880.* New York, S. A. Russell, 1935.

———. *The Souls of Black Folk.* New York, Fawcett Publications, 1964.

Edelstein, Tilden G. "John Brown and His Friends," in Hugh Hawkins (ed.), *The Abolitionists, Immediatism and the Question of Means.* Boston, D. C. Heath, 1964.

Elkins, Stanley M. *Slavery: A Problem in American Institutional and Intellectual Life.* New York, The Universal Library, Grosset & Dunlap, 1959.

Essien-Udom, E. U. *Black Nationalism: A Search for an Identity in America.* Chicago, University of Chicago Press, 1962.

Fanon, Frantz. *Black Skin, White Masks.* New York, Grove Press, 1967.

———. *A Dying Colonialism.* New York, Grove Press, 1967.

———. *Toward the African Revolution.* New York, Monthly Review Press, 1967.

———. *The Wretched of the Earth.* New York, Grove Press, 1966.

Farmer, James. *Freedom—When?* New York, Random House, 1965.

Fishell, Leslie H., Jr., and Benjamin Quarles. *The Negro American.* New York, William Morrow, 1967.

Fortas, Abe. *Concerning Dissent and Civil Disobedience.* New York, The New American Library, 1968.

Franklin, John Hope. *The Emancipation Proclamation.* New York, Doubleday, 1963.

———. *From Slavery to Freedom.* 3d ed. (revised and enlarged). New York, Alfred A. Knopf, 1967.

———. *Reconstruction After the Civil War.* New York, Oxford University Press, 1967.

Frazier, Edward Franklin. *The Negro Family in the U. S.* New York, The Dryden Press, 1948.

———. *Black Bourgeoisie.* New York, Macmillan, 1962.

Fromm, Erich. "Creators or Destroyers?" *Saturday Review,* 47 (Jan. 4, 1964).

Genovese, Eugene D. "The Legacy of Slavery and the Roots of Black Nationalism," *Studies on the Left,* 6 (November–December, 1966), 3–24.

———. *The Political Economy of Slavery.* New York, Random House, 1967.

Gerassi, John. *The Great Fear in Latin America* (rev. ed.). New York, Collier, 1965.

Guevara, Ernesto Ché. *Ché Guevara Speaks.* New York, Grove Press, 1967.

———. *Guerrilla Warfare.* New York, Alfred A. Knopf and Random House, 1968.

Hamilton, Alexander, *et al. The Federalist.* New York, Modern Library.

Harrington, Michael. *The Other America.* New York, Macmillan, 1963.

Hill, Herbert. "The Racial Practices of Organized Labor—The Age of Gompers and After," in Ross and Hill (eds.), *Employment, Race and Poverty.* New York, Harcourt, Brace & World, 1967.

Johnson, Charles S. *The Economic Status of Negroes.* Nashville, Fisk University Press, 1933.

Johnson, James W. *Along This Way: The Autobiography of James Weldon Johnson.* New York, The Viking Press, 1933.

Josephson, Matthew. *The Robber Barons*. New York, Harcourt, Brace & Company, 1934.

Kahn, Tom. *The Economics of Equality*. New York, League of Industrial Democracy, 1964.

Killens, John Oliver. *Black Man's Burden*. New York, Trident Press, 1965.

King, Martin Luther, Jr. *Stride Toward Freedom*. New York, Harper & Row, 1958.

Kinoy, Arthur. "The Constitutional Right," *Rutgers Law Review*, 21 (Spring, 1967), 396.

Lundberg, Ferdinand. *America's 60 Families*. New York, The Citadel Press, 1946.

Lynd, Staughton. *Reconstruction*. New York, Harper & Row, 1967.

McKissick, Floyd B. *Constructive Militancy*. New York, Congress of Racial Equality pamphlet, December, 1966.

———. *A Black Manifesto*. New York, Congress of Racial Equality pamphlet, July, 1967.

———. *Genocide*. New York, Congress of Racial Equality pamphlet, July, 1967.

McPherson, James M. *The Negro's Civil War*. New York, Random House, 1965.

Malcolm X, with Alex Haley. *The Autobiography of Malcolm X*. New York, Grove Press, 1965.

Mannix, Daniel P., and Malcolm Cowley. *Black Cargoes: A History of the Atlantic Slave Trade*. New York, Viking Press, 1962.

Meyer, Howard N. *Colonel of the Black Regiment*. New York, W. W. Norton, 1967.

Mills, C. Wright. *The Power Elite*. New York, Oxford University Press, 1956.

Myrdal, Gunnar. *An American Dilemma*. 2 vols. New York, Harper & Brothers, 1944.

National Committee of Negro Churchmen. "Black Power." Advertisement in *The New York Times*, July 31, 1966.

Nkrumah, Kwame. *I Speak of Freedom*. New York, Frederick A. Praeger, 1961.

Olmstead, Frederick Law. *The Slave States* (ed. by Harvey Wish). New York, G. P. Putnam, 1959.

Peck, James. *Freedom Ride*. New York, Simon and Schuster, 1962.

Poussaint, Alvin F. "The Negro-American: His Self-Image and Integration," *Journal of the National Medical Association*, 58 (November, 1966), 419–23.

Price, Hugh Douglas. *The Negro and Southern Politics: A Chapter of Florida History*. New York, New York University Press, 1961.

Quarles, Benjamin. *The Negro in the American Revolution*. Durham, University of North Carolina Press, 1961.

Rodney, Walter. *West Africa and the Atlantic Slave Trade*. Nairobi, Historical Association of Tanzania, East Africa Publishing House, 1967.

Ruchames, Louis, ed. *The Abolitionists: A Collection of Their Writings*. New York, Capricorn Books, 1963.

———. *A John Brown Reader*. New York, Abelard-Schuman, 1959.

Russell, Bertrand. "An Outline of Intellectual Rubbish," in *Unpopular Essays*. New York, Simon and Shuster, 1950.

———. "Ideas that have harmed mankind," in *Unpopular Essays*. New York, Simon and Shuster, 1950.

Tussman, Joseph, ed. *The Supreme Court on Racial Discrimination*. New York, Oxford University Press, 1963.

United States Commission on Civil Rights. *Enforcement—A Report on Equal Protection in the South*. Washington, D.C., Government Printing Office, 1965.

Walker, David. *An Appeal to the Coloured Citizens of the World*. New York, Hill & Wang, 1965.

Washington, Booker T. *Up From Slavery, An Autobiography*. New York, Doubleday, Page & Co., 1901.

Weisbord, Robert G. "The Back to Africa Idea," *History Today* (London), XVII (January, 1968).

Williams, Eric. *Capitalism and Slavery*. New York, Capricorn, 1966.

Woodward, C. Vann. *The Strange Career of Jim Crow*. New York, Oxford University Press, 1957.

Ziegler, Benjamin M., ed. *Desegration and the Supreme Court*. Boston, D. C. Heath & Co., 1958.

Zinn, Howard. *Albany, A Study in National Responsibility*. Atlanta, Southern Regional Council, 1962.

———. "The Limits of Nonviolence," *Freedomways*, 4 (First Quarter, 1964), 143–48.

———. *SNCC, the New Abolitionists*. Boston, Beacon Press, 1964.

# Index

racism in, 57
on slavery, 10, 57-58
social change and, 51-96
U.S. Supreme Court, 10, 36
racism and, 74-78
role of, 17, 51-96
Universal Negro Improvement
Association, 125, 126
University of Mississippi, 74,
139-140
University of Texas Law School,
94
Urban League, 141

Vanderbilt, Cornelius, 85
Vietnam War, 10, 41-42, 132,
133, 136, 158
U.S. and, 32-33

Voter registration, 37
Voters Rights Bill of 1965, 37

Washington, Booker T., 120,
124, 125, 126
Atlanta speech (1895), 118-
119
Washington, George, 59, 115-
116
Walker, David, 111, 112-113
West, E. Gordon, 88

Yarbrough (Klan cases), 73-74

Ziegler, Benjamin Munn, 60
Zinn, Howard, 55, 88
Zionist movement, 125

## DATE DUE

| NOV 9 '87 | | | |
|---|---|---|---|
| | | | |
| | | | |
| | | | |
| | | | |
| | | | |
| | | | |
| | | | |
| | | | |
| | | | |
| | | | |
| | | | |
| | | | |
| | | | |
| | | | |
| | | | |
| GAYLORD | | | PRINTED IN U.S.A. |